Over the
RAINBOW

FROM THE DEPTHS OF GRIEF TO HOPE

Sheila Clemenson

Copyright © 2023 by Sheila Clemenson

All rights reserved. No part of this publication may be reproduced, distributed, or transmitted in any form or by any means, including photocopying, recording, or other electronic or mechanical methods, without the prior written permission of the publisher, except in the case of brief quotations embodied in critical reviews and certain other noncommercial uses permitted by copyright law. For permission requests, write to the publisher at the address below.

Sheila Clemenson/Transitions Coaching Services, LLC
357 McCaslin Blvd #200
Louisville, CO 80027

sheilaclemenson.com

Disclaimer: The information contained in this book is for general information and entertainment purposes only. The recommendations, opinions, experiences, observations, or other information contained herein is provided "as is" and neither the author nor publisher make any representations or warranties of any kind, express or implied, about the accuracy, suitability, reliability, or completeness of this book's content. Any reliance a reader places on such information is therefore strictly at their own risk. All recommendations are made without guarantee on the part of the author and publisher. To the maximum extent permitted by law, the author and publisher disclaim all liability from this publication's use. In no event will either author or publisher be liable to any reader for any loss or damage whatsoever arising from the use of the information contained in this book. This book is not a substitute for professional services, and readers are advised to seek professional aid in the event of an emergency.

Ordering Information:
Quantity sales. Special discounts are available on quantity purchases by corporations, associations, and others. For details, contact the publisher at the address above.

Over the Rainbow/Sheila Clemenson. — 1st ed.
ISBN 979-8-218-27739-0

Dedicated to my husband Shawn.
You are my Over the Rainbow.

CONTENTS

Introduction xiii

CHAPTER 1: An Ocean of Feelings 1

CHAPTER 2: Waves of Grief 25

CHAPTER 3: It Takes an Island 43

CHAPTER 4: The Life Jacket: Self-Love and Worthiness 63

CHAPTER 5: Parting Clouds: Forgiveness and Hope 79

CHAPTER 6: Riding the Wave: Rebirth and Transformation ... 97

CHAPTER 7: Like Rain and Sunshine: Embracing the Future 119

CHAPTER 8: Winds of Change 139

CHAPTER 9: The Erupting Volcano: Unbelievable Losses 155

CHAPTER 10: Over the Rainbow: Gratitude, Resilience, and Joy 169

References 183

Acknowledgments 187

FOR YOU:

May the sun kiss your face and dry your tears
May a gentle breeze caress your cheek
like the touch of your loved one
May your peaks sustain you through your valleys
May you walk with footprints on the beach
and know you are not alone
May the intensity of the waves subside
to exhilarate and refresh you
And may you see your loved one's smile in every rainbow.

—Sheila Clemenson

Visit SheilaClemenson.com to purchase your copy of the
Over the Rainbow Companion Journal.

This resource is a cathartic way of processing your emotions and experiences. It takes you down memory lane by asking thought-provoking questions and sharing helpful suggestions.

PRAISES FOR *OVER THE RAINBOW*

"I've been waiting for this book for most of my life! Having experienced the loss of loved ones many times since an early age, navigating the feelings of anger, guilt, sadness, and grief can be so challenging and self-destructive. Sheila has created an invaluable guide that gently leads one to facing and healing the overwhelming feelings that often overshadow everything in one's life, most importantly self-care. Her courage and vulnerability in the telling of her story brought me to tears. Mahalo Nui."

—Carol Hart
carolhart.org

"Sheila Clemenson's book, *Over the Rainbow: From the Depths of Grief to Hope*, is simply phenomenal. It's a masterpiece that is strong in its purpose. From page one, I felt like I was riding the waves of Sheila's incredible journey right along with her. The *Companion Journal*, guided meditations, and playlists are incredibly well thought out as they are additional healing modalities not to be missed! Sheila peels away the layers of grief in such a relatable way. Her story is one of emerging from the brutal to find the beautiful. This book has touched me in such a meaningful way. I love that Sheila so pointedly lets her readers know and believe that we are never alone. This is a book to be shared, discussed, and treasured forever."

—Amanda Hoying
Wise Vibrations™, LLC Founder
Certified Chakradance™ Facilitator
Accredited Mindful Eating Guide
International Institute for Complementary Therapists Member
wisevibrations.com

"I loved how Sheila embraced every situation and threw herself into the moment. She learned from every lesson and continues to inspire others as she transforms herself. She shares an openness to all perspectives and energies, and doesn't shut ideas down, but lets them grow until she is ready. Sheila is an artist sharing her experience to support and help others."

—Stephanie Schacht
Attorney-At-Law, Estate Planning and Small Business Services
stephanieschachtlaw.com

"*Over The Rainbow* is not only an intimate look at the stages of grief, but also the stress and challenges of being a caregiver. Sheila takes the reader on her journey of falling in love with Grant, him being diagnosed with a fatal disease, and how she survived the grief and has transformed her life experiences into helping others. Sheila's encouragement to "make time to feel your feelings, giving yourself time and space to process them without judgment" resonates deeply. Any reader who is dealing with the death or illness of a loved one will find comfort with the positive messages and actual strategies presented. The structure of the book will allow readers to find and use the resources when they themselves are ready. I recommend this book to anyone who has lost an important person in their life or is currently a caregiver to a loved one. Sheila shares her experience of being widowed at a young age in a relatable way to help others cope with grief and the eventual acceptance that life can be fulfilling and happy even if it is not the life you originally planned."

—Leslie Algozin
Lifelong Friend and English Language
Arts Middle School Teacher, Lombard, IL

"Having gotten to know Sheila from her early years on Kauai with Grant, living their life out as a courageous couple with a huge appetite for life and an almost revengeful attitude towards the incurable path of ALS, I am deeply touched to read the journey from the depths of grief to hope that she has lived. This is a book that has demanded a life to be lived in all its colors and shades to come into being. The dedication the author has shown to personally face the turmoil of grief and share it in writing from a place of truly lived experience is what makes this book a gem. Though the author writes very personally, we can recognize ourselves in the very essence of the grieving anatomy. What also makes this book more than hopeful to read is how the author is actually holding each and every person that has touched her life in a light of grace and unity, true to the spirit of aloha! Be it a friend or a foe, she owns her own experience and embraces each contributor. This is how the book is one of hope and reminds us that we might feel alone yet we are never all alone on our journey through grief and rediscovery of life!"

—Anne-Kristine Tischendorf
Oslo, Norway

INTRODUCTION

THE PURPOSE OF THIS BOOK is to help grievers feel supported, validated, encouraged, inspired, and hopeful that they can move forward through their grief journey successfully. I see and know how vulnerable and raw you might feel. You may have lost your most valuable person (MVP), your identity as a caregiver, and so much of what made you who you are. This book is a beacon of support to be used in partnership with a grief therapist, grief wellness coach, and/or grief support community, to help you through emotionally processing grief: from falling into the grief pit, to climbing your way out, to finally finding hope. You're encouraged to explore a renewed sense of purpose and to feel joy again, in your own time.

I lived in the grief pit for what seemed like a lifetime, and I will never forget how it feels. I know you can climb your way out to feel the warmth of the sun again and perhaps see what I call "rainbows" and other mystical surprises that remind you that you are not alone.

I invite you to be open-minded as I guide you through my own grief journey with suggestions and exercises to support your grief process. By sharing my experience and how I found my way out to a supportive new life, I want you to know that you are not alone. May you find connection, validation, understanding, and self-discovery through your own grief experience, as different as it might be from mine.

You will find your way to the other side of your deep experience of grief. As grief becomes your companion and you learn to live with it, you will begin to see your experiences in a new way. You can learn how to forgive yourself and others while finding new meaning and purpose. And you can explore ways to bring your relationship with your loved one forward over time and through life changes, because they will be a part of your heart and life forever.

You will explore how to:

1. Identify your grief needs and learn how to practice "Radical Self-Care and Resourcing."
2. Navigate the roller coaster of complicated emotions and intense grieving.
3. Become a more conscious caregiver of yourself and others.
4. Manage your boundaries and grief around people, places, and things.
5. Forgive your own mistakes. Accept your humanness and try your best to do this for the important relationships in your life.
6. Explore managing your expectations of yourself and the expectations you hold of your loved ones.
7. Rediscover who you are now and explore reinventing yourself.
8. Build new relationships and bring new love into your life.
9. Embrace a new sense of hope, meaning, and purpose.
10. Build a stronger community, connections, and supportive relationships.
11. Trust in your ability to move forward, living each day in gratitude, resilience, and joy.

In your own way, you will work on coming to terms with what your life is without your loved one. By holding on to their memory, you can continue

INTRODUCTION

to have your own special relationship with them. You may find you have these mystical experiences—"rainbows"—that surprise you and can bring a sense of awe like we might feel upon seeing a physical rainbow. In the book, we'll consider how you experience these rainbows in your day-to-day life. You'll have the opportunity to explore by recognizing and interpreting the new language your loved one might be using to communicate with you from the other side. If you haven't experienced something like this yet, it doesn't mean you won't.

I've created a companion journal to go with *Over the Rainbow* as an idea from my own personal experience. For grievers who love to journal or write, as I did, it is a cathartic way of processing your emotions and experiences. It takes you down memory lane by asking thought-provoking questions and sharing suggestions of things that might be helpful. You can take the journal to your therapy sessions to share whatever you've been experiencing since your loved one died. I've also given you "Self-Reflection" at the end of each book chapter as an opportunity to explore more about your grief process, in addition to ideas for moving forward.

The *Over the Rainbow Companion Journal*, guided meditations, and Spotify playlists are available on my website at SheilaClemenson.com.

My story begins, ends, and continues in connection with Secret Beach, a place in Hawai'i that is near and dear to my heart. The waves, known as *nalu* in the Hawaiian language, are intense at this beach. Waves serve as a strong metaphor for emotions. In this book I refer to "grief waves." Like emotions, waves come and go on their own and give us the opportunity to reflect upon our life, experiences, and memories. They are a recurring theme throughout a personal grief journey, and this book.

OVER THE RAINBOW

OUR SECRET BEACH

> "Life is not measured by the number of breaths you take but by the moments that take your breath away."
>
> — *Maya Angelou*

It was the morning of September 4, 1999. As we got him dressed, I asked Grant, "Do you know where we're going today?" He nodded his head "yes" with the sweetest smile. He could only communicate with blinks and this small nod. When I said, "I'm making good on my promise to you—we're going to Secret Beach," my 36-year-old husband's eyes twinkled.

Our relationship began in 1992, when an old friend told me she had this terrific guy for me to meet—great personality, charismatic, and charming. "I don't think it will be a love connection," she said, "but you'll have fun."

It wasn't love at first sight, but Grant was the most sensitive, caring, and respectful man I had ever met. And the funniest! He always told a great joke that I had never heard before.

Three months later, Grant was promoted and told he would move to Paris in six months for an indefinite time. When I found out, I thought, *Isn't that just my kind of luck?* I was already head over heels in love.

We continued our relationship during those six months, but then he left for Paris, and I was in Detroit. For a year and a half, we saw each other every three months. We had international phone bills the size of mortgage payments and phone sex that would put the 1-900 numbers out of business. In September 1994, unable to take the separation any longer, I quit my job and moved to Paris.

INTRODUCTION

Paris really is for lovers. Where else can you experience the majesty of the Eiffel Tower while kissing the one you love in the moonlight? We also were able to travel to England, Ireland, Germany, and Switzerland between Grant's business trips. It seemed too good to be true.

Grant's company moved him back to the U.S. in December 1994. We decided to live together. I knew I wanted to spend the rest of my life with him, marriage proposal or not.

Grant began having problems walking in spring 1995. I remember him saying, "Watch me walk. Do I look funny?" It wasn't obvious at the time, but his left foot dragged when he walked or ran. He decided to see an orthopedic specialist, thinking his knees might have been damaged from a lot of skiing, but held off until after our long-awaited vacation to Hawai'i. I was excited to see Hawai'i for the first time, but I had no idea just how special this vacation would be.

On our first day, Grant took me to his favorite beach on Kauai, known as Secret Beach. We had to hike down a long, steep dirt trail, but Grant held my hand and coached my footing. After about 10 minutes, I saw the most brilliant aqua-blue ocean. As I got comfortable on my towel, Grant caressed lotion onto my back. I closed my eyes, finally relaxing in the 80-degree heat. Grant said, "I know it's hot, honey, but you really should slip something on." I looked up and noticed a small box on the towel in front of me. Before I could fully focus on what was happening, he opened the box and the most stunning, brilliant cut diamond engagement ring stared back at me. "Yes" was my answer. He had shaken my world and at the same time grounded me with his existence. I wanted to walk with him through life.

Three months later, on a muggy day in July, Grant came into the home we had bought as I was unpacking a box. He was unusually quiet and deep in thought. I greeted him with a hug and kiss and asked about his doctor's appointment. The orthopedic specialist had referred Grant to a neurologist when he found nothing wrong with his knees. Grant handed me some pamphlets, one about multiple sclerosis and the other about amyotrophic lateral sclerosis (ALS, also known as Lou Gehrig's disease) and said point-blank, "The doctor thinks I have one of these diseases. They are similar in symptoms and difficult to diagnose."

It took another four months to confirm Grant's diagnosis as Lou Gehrig's disease. The doctor told us it makes the nerves gradually die and no longer connect with the muscles. Eventually, people with ALS become unable to do anything for themselves and usually die within three to five years by choking or suffocating. The cause is unknown, and treatment is unavailable. Our dreams of a long life together were shattered.

Grant and I were in the midst of planning a Kauai wedding. He asked if I still wanted to marry him. I told him I had waited for him my entire life and I wanted to be together for as long as God was willing. When we married on March 24, 1996, repeating, "In sickness and in health for as long as we both shall live," our family and friends knew the gravity and determination behind our words.

Grant's health declined quickly. He spent most of his time in a wheelchair and it was getting more difficult to use his hands. We both agreed it was time for Grant to plan for early retirement. We had always dreamed of retiring in Kauai, but we never dreamed we would be in our 30s.

The native Hawaiians say the island of Kauai either accepts or rejects you. Grant and I were accepted with open arms. Everything for our October 1997 move fell into place, including an accessible home for Grant.

Our marriage barely survived the gradual progression of Grant's illness to each new stage. It was easy for Grant and me to love each other for all of our wonderful qualities, but the true test was loving each other in all of our ugliness. I lost a husband, and he lost a wife. I gained a "child," dependent on me physically in every way.

When Grant lost the ability to speak clearly, I was the only person who could understand some of his words. I knew I still loved him and would

INTRODUCTION

be there for him until the end. I assured him of this time and again when he was trying to push me away. He didn't want to put me through all of his pain.

Two months before Grant died, he was hospitalized with pneumonia and then went home with hospice. Before we left the hospital, he made me promise I would take him to Secret Beach one last time. Coming home was overwhelming. I was getting about three to four hours of sleep per night, and Secret Beach was the farthest thing from my mind.

I finally accepted that Grant was not going to recover from his pneumonia. He was getting weaker, losing more of his precious energy each day. One day I said to our good friend Anne-Kristine, or A.K. as we called her, "We have to get Grant to Secret Beach this week or it will not happen." She talked to some people in the surrounding area that day and returned home with good news. A man named Miles was a property manager for one of the owners who had private access on the only road to the beach. Miles understood how important this was to us, because he'd taken care of a woman for two years who died of cancer. He said he would try to arrange it for the upcoming Saturday, September 4, and would call us.

Grant's condition worsened during the week. He mostly blinked his eyes to communicate with me. I spent Friday preparing for a picnic, champagne toast, and special ceremony. We hadn't yet heard from Miles. I told Grant the next day would be a special one and he needed to conserve his energy.

Miles finally called Friday night at 11 p.m. He told us to meet him at the gate by noon.

Early Saturday morning, I packed the cooler and picnic basket and gathered our wedding pictures and some books from which I planned to read. I also brought the leis I had saved from our wedding day. It was Hawaiian tradition to toss them into the ocean wrapped in *ti* leaves. If they float out and don't return, it means your love will be as deep as the ocean and your burdens as light as the sea foam above.

Grant was having a very difficult day, with shortness of breath and weakness. It was truly now or never. Six friends and my assistant helped me load up the Blazer with everything, including Grant's oxygen, morphine pump, and medications. A.K. supported Grant's head while we drove.

We arrived at the gate a little after noon. Miles was there and we soon were on our way down. When we arrived, we parked on the sand. It took all of us to get the wheelchair settled in a perfect place, with Grant's feet planted in the warm sand. Beautiful Hawaiian music played while the picnic area was arranged. Our wedding pictures and leis were set out; the champagne was chilled. During it all, I could see Grant soaking up the essence of the day.

After a while, I began my little ceremony. First, I made a champagne toast for the day. Grant was able to savor a bit of bubbly. Second, I read a beautiful prayer from Marianne Williamson's *Illuminata*, to help him let go of what he could no longer control. I also read from Shakti Gawain's *Creative Visualization*. I expressed my heartfelt gratitude and love to Grant. I told him it was OK to let go if he was ready. Then I wrapped our wedding leis in the *ti* leaves and cast them far out beyond the lava rock. We watched as they floated farther away with the waves.

Grant wanted some time to sit by himself. I wondered what he was thinking as I watched him sitting with his eyes closed. I was thinking of the day he had proposed on that beach and about life without him.

When we arrived home at 4 p.m., Grant had more problems breathing. For the next three hours, A.K. and I struggled to ease Grant's breathing. Then, at around 7 p.m., Grant decided he was tired of fighting. He looked me in the eyes knowingly when I listened to his lungs and could hear they were full of mucus. I said, "Grant, I know your lungs are filling up and I don't think there is anything we can do." Then, all of a sudden, he gave me several eye blinks, which was our agreed-on signal that he was ready to leave. I held him and said, "Grant, I love you," and kissed him on the lips. Then I said, "You go on and get out of that body because it's not working

INTRODUCTION

for you anyway." And he was released. I could feel the presence of his love and warmth in the room.

I held him for four hours before they came for his body. I laughed and cried. I was so happy he was free of his prison, yet so sad for myself and others who were cheated out of more time with this wonderful man. I called some family and friends to tell them. A.K. and I lit candles and played the same music from the beach earlier that day. I didn't want the moment to end, because when it did, I knew I would only have my memories.

CHAPTER 1
An Ocean of Feelings

> "You are not a drop in the ocean. You are
> the entire ocean in a drop."
>
> — *Rumi*

THE NEXT DAY

I look into the mirror, hardly recognizing myself. I'm 31 years old, and I look so fucking old. My pale face is puffy and red, my almond brown eyes and stringy, "dirty blonde" hair far from the lightness of my usual sun-kissed highlights and inner being. For sure, a part of me has died.

Have I been trying to be who my husband wants me to be for so long that I don't know who I am anymore? With exasperation, I think, *Yes*. And I'm trying to find myself through the depths and layers of my own survival and grief. My personal fight with my late husband Grant's illness is finally over.

I'm standing naked in the shower with the water flowing over the tears in my eyes, holding on with everything that I've got, waiting for someone to shake me and tell me it's going to be OK. That I'm going to wake up from this awful nightmare, the death of my husband. I don't care how long I have been anticipating Grant's death. I never could have prepared myself for what this feels like. It's a punch deep to the gut; visceral. I feel like I'm going to throw up, not just once, but all of the time. I get out of the shower, drying myself off and wondering if I should try to make myself throw up, but decide against it.

I get dressed in a daze in our bedroom, then suddenly in a flash, I'm thinking about the moments before Grant died in this very room. Looking into his eyes and taking his last deep breaths in unison with him. Once, in the distant past, Grant had breathed with me. Many years before this time, Grant was in the emergency room with me while I was having an asthma attack. My breathing was focused and shallow. I remember him looking into my eyes and drawing each breath with me. I know in the very soul of my being that Grant understood in his final moments that I knew exactly what he was feeling as he gasped for each breath of air. And I will never forget how connected I felt to him in those final moments.

The doorbell rings, startling me, and as I answer the door in a hurry, I see two friendly faces staring back at me. They are my fairly new neighbors, Al and Marcy, from next door. Marcy is holding a gorgeous tropical floral arrangement and they both offer their sympathy. This is the first time we meet face to face, previously only passing by with a hand wave and smile while driving in and out of the compound where we live. When Grant was alive, he saw Al unpacking his truck one muggy afternoon and said, "Munchkin, have Holly get him a beer," so I called out to Holly in the kitchen, and she immediately walked out to Al offering a cold beer and a smile.

Little did I know at that time, but Al and Marcy would become an integral part of my island family, or *ohana* as it is called in Hawai'i. In fact, through them I connected with many of my lifelong friendships on Kauai. They embraced and emotionally looked after me, offering a home for special gatherings, unconditional love, and the laughter I so desperately needed in my life, with the best music-filled parties ever. Several dear friends lived on "the compound," as we called it over time, and it became a place to "talk story," a local Hawaiian term for what someone on the mainland might call "shooting the shit," and sharing aloha spirit. It became a trusting place filled with *ohana* that I needed then more than ever.

I decided to spend the day after Grant died by calling family and friends to share our news, well, my news. And the incredible experience I was blessed with on his last day. This was well before the time you could create a blanket posting for everyone to see on Facebook. And somehow, we all survived without it, but maybe it would have been far less exhausting than having consecutive conversations so many times. Yet I also realized these conversations and sharing our story of Grant's last day again and again became a healing balm for my soul.

Sleeping in our bed without Grant was lonely. I didn't want to sleep by myself, but I was so exhausted that I couldn't keep my eyes open. I didn't know if I was still thinking about Grant or lucid dreaming, but I kept reliving the events of the past 48 hours in my mind. I couldn't believe we successfully navigated his last wish. I smiled thinking about Secret Beach, this dream of Grant's that seemed so impossible. And I finally fell asleep.

MAGICAL MOTHER KAUAI, THE NURTURER

Note: What follows includes descriptions of wahi pana, which are sacred and celebrated places. Many people—including emergency rescue workers—have lost their lives in these places. Great respect for these sacred sites is essential, as they might be dangerous and should not be trespassed upon, especially if there are warning signs and gates to keep travelers out.

On Labor Day, two days after Grant's passing, A.K. wanted to take me on an adventure, a most magical Kauai day in my new life without Grant. Talking about where to go, we soon realized that there were a few hidden gems on the island, places I had never been, despite living there for years. She told me she had a few surprises for me, and I was intrigued. I had experienced tremendous guilt that I was the healthy one in my marriage. I had consciously and actively avoided flaunting my ability to do whatever I wanted without physical limitations. So much so, in fact, that I had gained more than a few unwanted pounds.

Reminiscing back in time, it is so funny how I met A.K. I walked in the front door of my home after a long day at work, greeting Grant upon my arrival, and he said to me, "Honey, this is Anne-Kristine from Norway. She's going to massage me in our bedroom while you watch her baby."

I saw this gorgeous Norwegian woman with the prettiest face, long flowing soft brown hair, blue eyes, and a dancer's body standing there, and wondered what planet I had landed on. Before I could say anything, she approached me with the warmest smiling eyes and said, "My husband, Arnt, is in the kitchen with Fridjtof."

This connection became the beginning of the most special friendship I could have ever imagined. This Norwegian beauty had approached Grant at Hanalei Bay as he sat in his wheelchair spending the day with his caregiver. She approached him because she wanted to do healing work with him. At that time A.K. was the owner of a massage practice in Norway and studied shamanism with Serge King of Aloha International on the North Shore, a network of teachers, counselors, massage therapists, and thousands of individual members. I have many stories of our times together, and she has proven herself to be my Earth angel, grounded and with a little dirt on her wings. She is from this world, but not of it.

We set out on our journey to the North Shore up to the beach at the end of the road, Ke'e Beach, one of my favorites on the island. Driving to the North Shore with the windows down always fills me with the scents of the 'aina, a Hawaiian word meaning the land and its produce as well as the sea and all that comes from it to sustain the people. I took it all in with the windows down, driving through Kilauea and the sensory overload of spectacular mountain views extending far beyond where one's eyes meet the valleys. Green, lush, and dense tropical forests line the two-lane highway, the only road taking you to the North Shore of the island.

VISIT TO THE HEIAU

When I met A.K., she had been practicing and dancing hula for a number of years. Hula is the storytelling dance of the Hawaiian Islands, and the practice is rich in Hawaiian history, genealogy, customs, traditions, and the tales of those who came before. From hula one learns about Hawaiian plants and flowers, and in this way, hula strengthens stewardship of the environment. Ferns, maile, and other flowers are gathered to make leis and costumes for the performance.

The *heiau* is a sacred temple created with stone and lava rocks. Some are simple structures built on level ground while others are elaborate terraces with multiple tiers. In ancient times, these might only be used for religious purposes by high chiefs (*ali'i*) or priests (*kahuna*). Others were used for ceremonial, healing, and agricultural purposes.

A.K. wanted to take me to the *heiau* at the end of the road—near Ke'e Beach at the edge of the Kalalau trail. There are two ancient sites on the far side of Ke'e Beach, and they are considered Kauai's most sacred spots—Ka Ulu a Paoa and Ke Ahu a Laka—associated with the ancient art of hula and the goddesses Laka and Pele.

Upon entering the *heiau*, we offered blessings to the goddesses and Mother Kauai. We breathed in the air of this sacred ground and place of tranquility. I could feel the energy in the tingling sensation of my bare feet against the earth, like an electrical current, vibrating with divine warmth and connection. This was a magical experience in a hidden gem of a location. A gift from Mother Kauai, the native spirits and plants that have lived for what must be forever in our concept of time. We enjoyed our connection with this sacred place and then gave a prayerful blessing of gratitude and "*a hui hou*," the Hawaiian phrase meaning until we meet again.

VISIT TO THE CAVE

Our next stop, Waikapalae Wet Cave, was also near Ke'e Beach. In the cave, waters glow blue in just the right sunlight, due to the light reflecting off the calcite rocks. It is a magical place, of course, discovered by Hollywood and featured in the movie "Pirates of the Caribbean: On Stranger Tides" as the Fountain of Youth. I didn't know at the time that there might be hazardous bacteria in the water, and it can be dangerous to swim in the dark if you don't have a headlamp. (The cave is currently closed, and access is not permitted.)

We stepped into the water and felt the shock of the coolness, which soon resulted in not feeling our feet touch the bottom. It felt like I was swimming in a dark void, very much like the grief pit I experienced, an everyday part of my life. A.K. and I held our breath, swimming underwater to enter the cave from below, and when we came back up about 10 seconds later, we found ourselves in the middle of this dark cave. We encountered other adventurers with underwater headlamps and cameras, yet we experienced the eerie darkness that surrounded us. It felt creepy and I had to manage my fears. My mind filled with thoughts of sea monsters from the deep, grabbing my feet and pulling me under. We didn't see any blue that day, and although we had sunny weather, it did not bring the magical azure colors we hoped to see. Perhaps it was more appropriate that I experienced the dark depths of the deep void that could swallow me whole. It was rather fitting for the emotions of the grief I found myself in.

VISIT TO QUEEN'S BATH

Our final sacred site visit for the day was to Queen's Bath, located at the end of a cul-de-sac in a residential subdivision in Princeville where parking is a challenge. The dirt path leads to a potentially dangerous tide pool in a bed of lava rocks with a supply of ocean water, as the tide waves break onto the land to replenish it. For many months of the year, it is not safe to visit. We visited at a safe and low tide time in early September.

Queen's Bath, formerly called Keanalele, was used by native Hawaiians for royal bathing and relaxation. We were able to park near the entrance and found our way along a slick, muddy trail. I walked diligently with focused attention to my footing to ensure I didn't slip and fall. We came upon a refreshing waterfall amidst foliage and flowers as we approached the bottom of the trail.

Conditions were calm on this day, so we trekked across the lava rocks, making sure we stayed away from the edge of the ocean. We watched out for any potential breaking waves and stayed in the drier areas. There were some slippery spots, and I was vigilant about where I took my next steps. At the entry point stood a carved sign with the words "Queen's Bath Drownings" at the top, tally marks beneath them to indicate the number of deaths that had occurred, and a matter-of-fact message after that of "Unexpected large waves will knock you off rocks and sweep you out to sea."

Upon entering the area we came upon the "Pool of Death," as it is referred to. As we walked near the edge, I caught a glimpse of three sea turtles swimming while searching for food. Was there a significance to seeing three sea turtles? I believed so. In Hawaiian culture, the Hawaiian sea turtle *honu* is a symbol of longevity, protection, and good luck. It also signifies *mana* or spiritual energy, and shows up in the form of *'aumakua*, a sacred ancestral guardian spirit offering protection, wisdom, and guidance. Suddenly it felt like Grant was there with me, giving me some kind of message that I was protected and safe. When we arrived at the protected lava rock swimming pool, I slipped into the calm waters of Queen's Bath, nurturing myself in the healing salts of the ocean, thinking about Grant being with me and finally experiencing this together. In my mind, I could make up whatever I wanted. In this moment, he was with me and more alive than he had been in years.

The day I spent with A.K. was exactly what I needed after the tremendous stress and intensity of the final days of Grant's life and his death. A.K. was a calming presence, which helped to ground me in a comforting and nurturing way. The sacred places we visited helped me to reconnect with Mother Kauai, feeling closer to the island than ever, rejuvenating my body and spirit.

PHONE CALLS AND PENNIES FROM HEAVEN

It first happened about a week after Grant died, when my mom was visiting from the mainland. We were driving from the North Shore beaches back to my home in Kapahi. The stationary car phone in the armrest console started ringing. I looked at my mom in surprise, mostly because we were on the North Shore and not only did no one call me on this phone, but calls didn't come through easily in that area. I couldn't remember anyone who had this number. I picked up the handset and answered, "Hello?" There was a long stretch of static on the line and then the phone went dead.

The funny thing is, the moment the phone rang, my mom and I were talking about Grant. It was probably some crazy story about a hilarious thing he did. We had a lot of these stories. After I hung up the phone, Mom and I looked at each other and I said, "Do you think it was him?" and we smiled.

The next time this happened was a few weeks later. I was talking to Grant's former caregiver, Holly, who had become a close friend and my new roommate. I told her about how the house phone kept ringing, and every time I answered it, I heard pure static on the line. And then suddenly, as we spoke about everyday stuff, the phone rang. I looked at her and she glanced at me. She went to pick it up, answering as she had many times while in our home caring for Grant. She handed it to me. And it was static! She said, "Yes, it's Grant. He has these phone calls from the other side down."

I said, "He's probably frustrated as hell that he can't actually talk to us and tell us about his new adventures."

It wasn't a secret to me that Holly had psychic abilities. I knew I could share this with her, as she had shared other psychic thoughts with me while she was a caregiver for Grant. One time when she was watching over Grant in the hospital before he came home with hospice, she asked him, "Grant, do you have a friend from Scotland who died?" Grant shook his head "No" and didn't say another word. When she brought it to my attention later that one of Grant's friends was trying to reach out from the other side, she asked me the same thing. I said, "No, but he has a friend named Scott who died." And Holly said, "Well, that's who it is." She just hadn't thought the name would be so obvious.

I stood up with Scott, Grant's friend, in the wedding of the couple who would set up Grant and me. This was about a year before we went on our first date. Scott had diabetes in its most debilitating form. He was unable to move his legs and he needed to use a wheelchair. I was the bridesmaid responsible for maneuvering his wheelchair down the processional line in the church. Little did I know, but Grant told me later he had admired me from a distance while sitting among the wedding guests. He shared about how much it meant to him that I supported his friend Scott that evening, making him feel comfortable. I've thought about that experience as it foreshadowed what was to come in our life together.

Holly and I had been through serious shit together, caring for "my invalid," as Grant jokingly referred to himself. Holly came into our lives by answering an ad for a caregiver in the local paper. She is six feet tall and a stunning surfer babe model with tattoos, and the most beautiful green eyes and big smile. With darkly tanned skin and every bit of aloha spirit, she walked into our home wearing cut-off shorts and a pretty Hawaiian-themed shirt decorated with a sparkling hula dancer.

I distinctly remember Grant asking her, "You know this job is going to require a drug test, right?"

Holly said, "Well, I'm going to tell you right now that I'm going to fail it."

Grant said, "You didn't even ask what the test is…because it's how fast can you roll a joint?"

As they laughed together, in that instant, I knew she was a part of our *ohana*.

The final time I received his static phone call was about six weeks after Grant died, when I was in northern Michigan visiting with a mutual friend of ours while planning his memorial service in Charlevoix. I told her I was receiving these static phone calls from him. And I'm dead serious, not a moment after telling her this, her landline phone rang. She answered it and there indeed was static on the line again! No one else was home to play a joke on us. Remember, we didn't have cell phones in 1999, like we do today. Cue the *Twilight Zone* theme!

At this time, I also started to get "pennies from heaven." Grant started sending me pennies. I would find them on the ground, in the car, around the house, or even out in public. When I picked them up the dates would match different significant years for us, like 1996, when we got married. Or 1992, the year we went on our first date. Sometimes I found them in the most random places. I told him he could send me $50 bills with President Grant on them. I'm still waiting for these.

THE ZOLOFT SMILE

Grant and I had a magnet on our fridge: a person with pearly whites beaming and the words, "The Zoloft Smile." Grant got it from one of the nurses at the ALS clinic, probably because he saw it and asked for one. He had a special way of just knowing what we needed in the moment to lighten our day. He was filled with an arsenal of comic relief in that twisted brain of his and God knew we were going to need it.

It was 1996, and we had both been on Zoloft since Grant's diagnosis a year earlier. I'm not sure what took us so long to come to terms with taking this, one of the best antidepressants around; maybe we felt like it was some kind of crutch that strong people didn't need. We needed anything that could even remotely help with the emotional roller coaster we were on, and we'd finally realized it. We were properly medicated and armed to stumble around in the dark of our emotions looking for a light switch.

But maybe we needed anti-nausea medicine as well, because everyday life was becoming one hell of a white-knuckle ride. When we weren't pretending everything was FINE (remember, this means Fucked up, Insecure, Neurotic, and Emotional), we were crawling into bed holding on to each other and crying our eyes out for hours. And this is no exaggeration.

I took Zoloft for more than five years; I'm not a medical doctor, but I highly recommend it. As hard as it was for me to manage the side effects of finally getting off of it many years later, I'm sure it had a lot to do with me surviving my caregiving and intense grief. At any given time, I didn't even want to think about getting off Zoloft. I numbed myself with this prescribed medication, some self-prescribed recreational drugs, and, of course, a lot of alcohol in the first few years of my post-death grief journey. Probably the very things one shouldn't do. I don't recommend any of *that*, but this was my dysfunctional reality with toxic coping strategies.

TAKE YOUR INVALID TO WORK DAY

Grant called it "Take your invalid to work day" when I needed to take him with me to the Taro Fields clothing store at the Marriott because we didn't have a caregiver for the day. It was a refreshing break for Grant, a major extrovert, to be out with the public. It was an opportunity for him to talk with people and hang out. Something different for him to do that day.

For me, it couldn't have made my life more stressful. I needed to attend to his needs *and* take care of customers. I found myself resentful because "work" was my escape from our everyday reality. And our reality was hitting me smack in the face on this particular day.

Grant was experiencing a difficult day physically, with bowel issues. With a moment's notice, I needed to close the door for the store and put the sign up that I would be back in 10 minutes, as I was the only sales associate there for most of the hours on my shifts. At first, it seemed nothing was going right. I couldn't maneuver his wheelchair through the store and kept bumping into clothing hangers and knocking dresses to the floor. When I needed to lock the doors, a couple wanted to come in and I had to tell them I would be back as soon as possible because "nature was calling." Anything that could go wrong, did. Another time later that day, I was frustrated beyond belief. As we went through this drill one more time, I said out loud, "This is why I go to work—to get away from this shit!"

The moment the words slipped out of my lips, I knew I couldn't take them back. The look on Grant's face said it all. I will never forget the pain and tears in his eyes. Why couldn't I just keep my damn mouth shut and carry on?

After Grant died, the guilt from this experience and others gnawed at me and left me with a pit in my stomach. I would replay this and other experiences in my mind while trying to fall asleep or at different times throughout the day when I would go off into another world, the life I used to have with Grant. I didn't know if these remorseful feelings would ever go away. I felt awful about these challenging times when I would jump into anger as a first line of defense, fighting an invisible enemy who had taken over my husband's body, yet taking it out on him.

THE REVEREND CARRIE CARTER: ANGEL VISION, FENTON, MICHIGAN

About six months before Grant died, a customer entered as I worked at the Taro Fields clothing store at the Marriott. Striking up conversations was easy for me, but this was especially easy because this person was a fellow Michigander. I can't remember how we got on the subject of psychics, but I had written in my journal I carried with me at the time that she recommended

I reach out to the Reverend Carrie based in Fenton on my next trip to Michigan.

I didn't remember this until well into my trip to Michigan in October 1999, when I was planning Grant's memorial service in Charlevoix. I pulled out my journal and started mapping out my plan. As I turned the pages, I stumbled upon my note to self. There was even a phone number. I decided to call and ask for an appointment. The receptionist said, "I'm sorry, but we're booked out three months in advance … Oh, wait, we just got a cancellation for November 4th—would you like 4 p.m. that day?"

The fourth happened to be the day before I was flying back to Kauai, so I said absolutely!

It had been a full month of visiting our close family and friends. My heart was filled with love, stories, nurturing, and all the special memories of past times shared together. Some stories I hadn't yet heard, while others I knew intimately. Grant had built a robust network of friends, and it made me feel closer to him in ways that are hard to describe. It was almost like I had another life with him so long ago when he was much younger and healthier. When these heartfelt times came to an end, I finished my trip by visiting with Grant's best friend Darv one last time for dinner, but not before I went for my appointment with the Reverend Carrie.

Entering Angel Vision, the Reverend Carrie's office, I tried to prepare myself for what this experience might hold. I couldn't have imagined what she would share with me. Remember, this was before anyone could look you up on Google. So it was harder for people to know things about you in advance with just a little bit of research. When I walked in and sat down, I saw a beautiful blonde woman, who looked very much like Sylvia Browne, a psychic medium and author appearing regularly on *The Montel Williams Show* and *Larry King Live*. She sat at a desk across from me and began, "Is there someone named Richard you are waiting to hear from?" I told her that I didn't know anyone named Richard. However, thinking about this much later, and after my experience with Holly and Scott/Scotland, I realized that perhaps she had heard from Frederick, my biological father, who died when I was 5 years old. Without hesitation, she went on to the next subject and began talking about my deceased husband.

There wasn't much she couldn't have guessed, until she looked at me strangely and asked, "Was Grant afraid of going to the dentist?"

"No," I said, "Grant loved going to the dentist—getting the nitrous gas was something he considered fun when he visited his dentist, an old friend."

She replied, "Why is he telling me, 'Now I don't have to worry about going to the dentist'?"

My eyes grew huge because this is exactly what I had said to Grant about two weeks before he died. Grant was meticulous about being clean and had wanted a dental cleaning appointment scheduled. I had a long conversation with our dentist at the time and we decided the chance of him aspirating was too high to risk it with his breathing and swallowing difficulties. When I told Grant I wasn't going to schedule an appointment later that day, he was angry. He said it wasn't fair and then got shitty about it. As only a wife who had been through this debilitating illness for more than four years and with a husband in hospice could do, I said to him, "Grant, where you are going, you don't need your teeth! You don't need to worry about going to the dentist!"

And that was that. I was not entertaining the idea and put my foot down. He wasn't happy about it. Clearly, this was his way of telling me I was right. He didn't need to worry about going to the dentist, after all.

I shared my story with the Reverend Carrie and just cried. I asked for his forgiveness. She asked me, "Why do you think you need to be forgiven?" I told her how much we hurt each other verbally and how difficult it had been to walk this journey together. I was far from the perfect wife. And she looked at me, saying, "Grant says you are his Aphrodite. You have nothing to be sorry for. He adores you. And in your humanness—both of you—you were under great stress and pressure. He knows this isn't your heart. He says there is nothing to forgive, and he loves you."

In that moment I felt completely healed of the biggest weight of guilt on my heart. Suddenly, I felt a lightness I hadn't experienced since before Grant's ALS diagnosis. Knowing I had just connected with Grant on the other side, beyond a shadow of doubt, gave me inner peace.

THE HARDEST DECISION

Some might say it was courageous of me to marry Grant knowing he was diagnosed with ALS.

I would say I wasn't going to leave him and not go on this journey with him, when I had gone on so many others. I had waited my entire life for this extraordinary human, and I wasn't going anywhere. To venture into the unknown of Grant's illness and grow into the experience of living with it each day was the commitment that I made to him.

However, understanding something intellectually and living it are two different things. Ask any parent about their first newborn. Maybe they knew what it would be like. But they didn't really know until they experienced it. Yet, as babies grow, they become more independent. In our situation, Grant would only become more reliant upon me and his other caregivers, losing the ability to do everything for himself and slowly losing every part of his independence; what made him who he was through his personal expression.

Despite my unquestioning commitment to our relationship, it still blows my mind that I considered having a baby with Grant when we were newly-weds and only one year into his illness. I had some intense maternal urges at 27 years old, a short time after we got married, and intentionally got off the Pill. We didn't actively try to conceive, but I desperately wanted a part of Grant with me. I wanted to experience and to give him the experience of bringing a soulful human, a part of each of us, into our world. Selfishly, I wanted a part of Grant with me. And I would never apologize for wanting that.

When we were in the ICU at the end of Grant's life, he asked me if I wanted to freeze his sperm as an option to have his baby after his death. When I could devote my life to this beautiful being. Every desire in me screamed, "Yes." But ultimately, I had to look him in the eyes with tears rolling down my face and tell him, "I'm sorry, but no." It was the hardest decision. I could not with everything in me bring a child into this world with even a remote chance of getting this dreadful disease. Since they didn't (and still don't) know what causes ALS, I wasn't taking any chances. Surely the only thing that would push me over the edge would be having and caring for a child with this murderous disease.

SWEET LITTLE SYDNEY

I was a caregiver for many years, and the house felt quiet and lonely two months after Grant died, when I returned from my travels to Michigan. I have always been an animal lover, and I knew I needed a fur baby. I went to Kauai Humane Society one afternoon, a trip to the other side of the island, to check out who was available.

When I walked into the room, I knew from the moment I saw him that he was mine. This cartoon character, a Jack Russell Terrier/Schnauzer mix named Seymour, stood on top of a barrier, barking at a cat in the distance. He had a spunky, fearless attitude, something I felt I could use a bit more of. I decided to adopt him. From the moment my little guy got in the car, he rested his head on my arm and kissed me while I was driving. He looked up at me with those eyes—the ones that said he was grateful to find his forever home. I re-named him Sydney, because he was running around with "a Sheila," the slang term for a gal they use in Australia.

A noteworthy fact: Australia and New Zealand were part of the trip of a lifetime that got away from Grant and me years ago when he was still working his international sales career. He broke his arm and we needed to cancel our five-week trip to both countries due to his complications with ALS.

Syd, as I called him, was a funny little dog. I gave him the middle name "Seymour Butts under the bleachers," because the name was perfect for his mischievous personality! Syd was with me for 15 years, and he lived in three desirable states; he hated road trips but loved many adventures. He lived his best life. There were times I thought Syd acted more like a human than a dog. It's funny to say this, but so many things Syd reminded me of Grant! I had a housewarming party in my new home on Noni Street and I put a bow tie on him. He greeted guests at the door with a short rawhide chewy that looked like a cigar. Grant loved cigars! I had parties all the time and he was quite the social butterfly, an opportunist who would take extra treats off guests' leftover plates. When I bought an exquisite box of chocolates from my last trip to Switzerland—Grant's favorite, Frigor—my cats knocked the pretty box all over the floor, after which Syd ate seven pieces before I discovered what had happened. I knew chocolate could be toxic to dogs, so I was concerned, but he appeared perfectly fine. The fascinating part was the way he ate the chocolates because it wasn't how a normal dog might eat them. Each chocolate was carefully unwrapped, the foil wrappers stacked on one another as if Syd was savoring each bite. What kind of dog eats chocolate like that?

There are other stories, like the time I had a baby shower for my good friend Terri, one of our caregivers who became my close friend. Syd decided to hump some of the women's legs when we were laughing about something, quite animated. Like it was his way of showing off and perhaps telling Terri he was happy for her, too! I have no idea if our deceased loved ones can visit us through animals, even for a short time, like an opening to experience this life and revisit us after they have passed. But many times I thought if Grant was a dog, he would be my Syd. Which is rather fitting when he used one funny "Grantism." When Grant couldn't talk very well anymore, he communicated the sweetest sentiment when he was happy and said, "If I had a tail it would wag." How cute is that? For some reason, I felt a little closer to Grant having Syd in my life.

THE MUSIC LOVER

Shortly after I brought Syd home, I was washing the floor on my hands and knees while jamming to some music. And out of nowhere, the music volume rose on its own to a deafening volume while playing "Lovesong" by The Cure. I yelled, "Holy shit, what the hell, Grant!"

I realized "The Grantster" appeared to be getting really good at interacting with all kinds of electrical connections. I had never experienced anything like this before, the phone ringing and now the stereo?! I jumped up and turned down the volume on the stereo, one of Grant's prized possessions. I listened to the radio, wondering how he knew the perfect song to send to me. The lyrics couldn't have been more perfect; it was as if he were singing them directly to me. This is the first of many songs that Grant has sent me, and he continues to do so even to this day.

INTO THE DEEP: JUNE 1968

Clark, Christianson, Clemenson—I wear my name like a badge of honor. I've come so very far since I was born Sheila Renee Clark. From a girl who lost her father at 5 years old to suicide, to growing up with my widowed mom who had gotten pregnant with me at 18 and not because she wanted to be. When she told my sweet, Polish and very Catholic grandma, the only girl of four who didn't become a nun, my grandma said, "Why didn't you just tell us you wanted to get married?"

Well, because she didn't. But that's what you did in 1968 when you were raised a proper Catholic girl. And this is how my life began. I was born on one of the hottest days in June that year, so unbearably hot that the air conditioning stopped working in the labor and delivery unit of the hospital in Detroit, Michigan.

REFLECTION

In the moments after Grant died, I immediately felt the emotional release of all of my responsibilities and the heavy burden I had carried as a caretaker of his needs, more present and immediate than my own with each shallow and labored breath he took. To feel the sadness and relief at the same time was guilt-inducing. For in the moment of Grant's passing, he was experiencing so much anger. We didn't believe he had the appropriate dose of morphine to support his ability to breathe more easily. It was a weekend and things happened fast.

We didn't have enough time to adjust his dose with hospice before the close of day on Friday. We were waiting for the pharmacist to arrive on weekend hours and, in fact, the pharmacist entered our home in the moment before Grant blinked his eyes in the manner he had planned in advance to tell me he was ready to pass on. In that angry moment, he let go of his fight for breath and life.

I know I will be forever grateful that I can scratch the itch on my face, wipe my face and tears, and easily walk to the bathroom and wipe myself. I can move throughout my day, going wherever I want or doing what I need to with independence. I can talk freely, laugh, dance, and fully express myself in who I am. I can eat what I want, exercise, and breathe normally as an asthmatic with medication. I will never take this for granted. When my friend complains about her husband's dirty socks on the floor, I know how lucky she is to have dirty socks on the floor. Because when we have our health, we have everything.

I prayed to God each day, *Please heal Grant of this ALS*. I was bargaining when I said, "You can take everything that we have, and we'll completely start over again with nothing but the shirts on our backs." I bargained and negotiated like I could talk my way out of this nightmare, this living hell that we had come to live in. I'm not sure why I thought not having anything and starting over again would be better, but this is where I was emotionally at this time in my life.

I knew I wasn't the only one in the family who was bargaining with God. Grant's dad, Pappy, asked God to give him ALS in place of Grant. Because he had already lived a long, beautiful, and happy life. Bargaining with God or whomever you pray to is very real. In addition to the anger that I felt about why it was happening to him and us, at some point after his diagnosis, I decided I wasn't going to talk with God because I felt abandoned.

I was raised Catholic, and my dad's family was Baptist. I was exposed to religious differences at a young age. Formal religion hasn't ever been my thing. However, I have a deep, soulful connection to God/Goddess/Great Spirit/Jesus/Holy Spirit/Universe, and I call Them by many names. I believe that many paths lead to God/Goddess/Great Spirit. I'm spiritual, but not religious. Although I highly respect people who are or aren't. Although for those atheists who don't believe in something more powerful out there, my stories might make you reconsider.

Self-Reflection

Identify your grief needs and learn how to do what I call "Radical Self-Care and Resourcing."

What does personal "Radical Self-Care and Resourcing" look like? Selfish? Bitchy? Whatever you need it to be. You need to own your self-care and learn how to ask for what you need. You need to reach out for your "lifelines" so you don't feel alone. But sometimes, you need to feel OK about being alone because this gives you the time you need to process your emotions and experiences.

How do you identify your needs when you feel numb? Find a way to get back into your body.

For quite some time I reflected upon everything I said or did and the impact it had on the outcome of Grant's death. I took an emotional inventory of all the things I had no control over, but this mental and emotional processing is a part of the healing process. You must go through it to get to the other side of the intense emotional pain. Respecting this process and nurturing your way through it is the key and perhaps the hardest part. There is no specific timetable or stage when it is complete and in truth, time does not heal all wounds. It might diminish your memory, or in some cases make your memories stronger.

Go to the *Over the Rainbow Companion Journal* to work on the following:

1. Identify and list your needs: physical, emotional, mental, and spiritual. Think about body, mind, and spirit. Share in your journal about your needs. You will find this section in the *Over the Rainbow Companion Journal* with suggestions.

2. Surround yourself with the people, places, and things that nurture you.

3. How do you do "Radical Self Care" to stay healthy throughout your grief process? This is what you do to take better care of yourself, such as getting more sleep, eating healthful and balanced meals, creating strong boundaries, etc.

4. How do you "Resource Yourself" to replenish your energy? This is what you do that helps to revitalize yourself, such as nature walks, meditation, hot baths, etc.

5. What do you need most today? This will be different from tomorrow and will shift and change with each passing day. What is happening for you right now?

6. Don't wait to do grief counseling or go through an Employee Assistance Program (EAP) with your company—do it now!

7. Hospice organizations offer free or donation-based programs; check out your local organizations.

8. Explore moving your body through things you like to do. Consider Grief Yoga® classes.

CHAPTER PLAYLIST/GUIDED MEDITATIONS

- "I Couldn't Love You More," Sade
- "Hold On," Sarah McLachlan
- "Silence," Delerium, featuring Sarah McLachlan
- "White Sandy Beach of Hawai'i," Israel "Bradda Iz" Kamakawiwo'ole
- "Lovesong," The Cure
- For guided meditations and a gallery of photos, visit SheilaClemenson.com.

RESOURCES

- *Atlas of the Heart,* Brené Brown, Ph.D., MSW
- *The Grief Recovery Handbook,* John W. James and Russell Friedman
- *On Grief and Grieving,* Elisabeth Kübler-Ross, M.D., and David Kessler
- *Visions, Trips, and Crowded Rooms,* David Kessler
- Grief.com, David Kessler

CHAPTER 2
Waves of Grief

"Let the waves carry you where the light can not."
— *Mohit Kaushik*

THE GRIEF PIT AND ROGUE WAVES

How did I navigate the ocean of complicated emotions? How did I manage my boundaries by protecting myself from those around me? I insulated or put myself out there as the extrovert I am, mostly by numbing myself in socially drinking, smoking pot, and having inappropriate sexual relationships with men.

I have never felt so vulnerable as I did in the first year alone after Grant's death. To put it in another perspective, it was like walking down the street naked, much like Cersei did in her walk of shame in the show *Game of Thrones*. I imagined onlookers pointing and poking me in the fleshy parts of my soft belly where I had a little more fat than I wanted anyone to see.

Of course, this wasn't real. No one was actually doing anything like this to me. I wasn't even walking around naked in public. But it perfectly describes the emotional rawness in every inch of my being. I ached on the inside, while I wore it on the outside with my bloody scratches and eczema-ridden skin.

They say our emotions are amplified in our skin. Well, I was a feverishly itchy, annoyed hot mess. And with all of that, I had fallen deeply into the "grief pit," a dark place in my psyche that felt as emotionally raw as my irritated skin. I shared this casually with those I knew as well as strangers I was talking to, especially if they were brave enough and took the chance to ask me how I was doing. I was uncomfortably transparent, and you'd better be ready for it, because you asked.

Some days, I found myself face down in the cold muddy grief pit, my body completely covered. Other days, I would be on my back with the dried mud on my face, but my backside steeping in it. Sometimes I heard an echo when someone called down to me. Other times, I might not hear them at all. Or perhaps one person's voice might hit me like fingernails on a chalkboard and shock me awake and present. At any point in time, I could take my emotional temperature based on where I was in the grief pit. I would think, *I'm climbing my way out today and feeling hopeful.* Or, *I'm sliding back down and barely holding on by the tip of a finger.* Further along in my grief process, I would say "I'm 50 percent of the way out, with my feet dangling over the dark void, but my back is feeling the sunshine," only to slide back into the depths of the pit the next day—or moment by moment for that matter. I called it being in the depths of grief, and it was harsh.

At some point, I climbed out of the grief pit with all of my might, and I stood looking down into it.

Then I stumbled onto the beach, feeling the sun's warmth. I caught a glimpse of reflective, calm waters on the horizon, and then a powerfully rogue wave from out of nowhere crashed onto the beach and knocked me down. But at some point, I always got back up, and that is the key.

GRIEF BRAIN IS REAL

I've never experienced anything like the intense grieving of Grant's passing and knowing I wouldn't be able to talk to him, hold him, and laugh with him in this human way ever again. I've never experienced anything like grief brain either. Wild things happen to your memory in grief, like a brain fog, the way you forget things and do strange shit. Like when I left my full Starbucks coffee on the roof of my car and drove away without a clue. Or when I put my purse in the fridge as I unloaded groceries and then searched around the house for an hour retracing my steps wondering where the hell it was because I'd come home with it, or did I?

That's nothing; here is my No. 1 grief brain story:

I traveled to Mackinac Island—off the Upper Peninsula of Michigan—from Charlevoix after Grant's third memorial service to visit my best friend, Dee, with her family. I enjoyed seeing her and meeting her newest little one. Honestly, not much else stands out to me but the old-time beauty of this island. No automobiles are allowed on Mackinac Island. You can experience its quaint atmosphere for yourself in the romantic movie *Somewhere in Time* with Christopher Reeve and Jane Seymour.

Before the end of my visit, I decided to ride in the back of a horse-drawn carriage, which caused me to have a severe asthma attack. I had no idea how allergic I was to horses, and my reaction was intense. After using my inhaler, my breathing improved. I was lucky to survive another learning experience. Note to self, no more enclosed carriage rides. After this experience, I looked forward to getting into my rental car after the ferry dropped me off.

The drive to meet my local friend for dinner in Petoskey was over an hour. I was in a hurry to get there because as usual, I was running late. I'm sure my family and friends would agree the phrase "Hawai'i time" must have been created for me. I got to the restaurant, and as I walked up to the table, I gave my friend a big hug. Then, I noticed something important sitting as clear as day on the table. It was the blue folder and planner I had been carrying around with me for the entire trip to Michigan! What the hell was happening? I didn't even know I was missing it!

My friend told me some people in the Mackinac Island parking lot had found it on the ground and picked it up. When they saw the important papers in it, including death certificates, they knew they needed to find the person it belonged to. The only information they found was what was written for today in the planner—the name of my friend, the restaurant, and the time I had planned to meet her there. I couldn't believe these Earth angels decided to drive all the way to Petoskey to make sure I got it back! I was disappointed they didn't stay for a thank you, but I'm sure they had other people to watch over. I was dumbfounded and began to feel like I needed a completely new level of being looked after in my grief. I can only imagine my guardian angels were flying in overdrive trying to keep up with me.

I think it took about six months for my grief brain to diminish and return to somewhat normal, except for a blonde moment here and there. I didn't think I would ever be "normal" again. That ship had sailed a long time ago. Unfortunately, my alcohol consumption also made more holes in my memory with occasional blackouts, too. It is hard to say how much better my memory would have been if I wasn't drinking, but I'm sure I would've felt physically better the next morning.

ANNIVERSARIES AND HOLIDAYS

For important anniversaries and holidays, I found it best to plan far in advance how I would spend that special day. I would start to plan about a month prior to the occasion. The closer it would get to the actual date, the more I would break down in tears. Especially if it was my or Grant's birthday. Valentine's Day was another hard one. I needed to take extra emotional care of myself. I would make reservations at a restaurant for a special dinner with friends and buy myself a lei or flowers. Whatever I did usually helped me to feel stronger on the day of that special event or occasion.

One Valentine's Day, my friend and roommate Holly came home with a dozen red roses for me. She told me Grant wanted her to get them for me. I had the biggest smile on my face every time I admired and smelled them while reading the card she wrote to go with them. Holly was truly my rock for the year after Grant died. I know not many people could handle being a roommate with an emotional basket case like myself at that time. I'm sure she has more karma in her jar than she has used up in this lifetime and I'm forever grateful to her.

Planning for the Christmas and New Year's holidays without Grant that first year was hard. I was so fortunate to have a compassionate and loving *ohana* who looked out for me and remembered me in special ways during those most difficult times. This is what got me through my hard grief. If I didn't have my *ohana*, my family and friends on the mainland to fall back on, as my silver lining—and there are many of them to thank in my life (you know who you are and how you showed up for me)—I don't know if I would be here right now.

SERVICES AND SCATTERING OF ASHES

How many memorial services do you have for someone who was in international sales and traveled extensively around the world? I had three—on Kauai at Secret Beach, in Charlevoix, Michigan, and in Leysin, Switzerland. Each one was special in its own way.

Half of Grant's ashes were scattered into the ocean's waves at Secret Beach about a week after he died. We had a close-knit group of friends at the beach in a gathering circle, sharing stories and memories of Grant and how much he meant to us.

The other half of his ashes were taken to La Berneuse, a mountain of the western Bernese Alps above Leysin where Grant lived in his twenties, enjoying as much skiing as possible while working at Hefti Sports for the best nine months of his 20-something life. A few European lifelong friends, including Grant's best friend Darv and myself, took the gondola to the top of the mountain where there was a restaurant with stunning views of the Swiss Alps and Lake Geneva. We gave Grant a proper adieu, but not before the amulet I was using to gather and keep a small portion of his ashes fell into his urn. I was embarrassed and needed to dip my hands in to find it. When I took my hands out, they shimmered a bit from his ashes.

As Darv and I scattered his ashes in the Alps, the wind kicked up all of a sudden, further spreading his ashes at just the right time to leave a slight glistening on my face and clothing. I didn't see this until I went to wash my hands in the restroom. Well, I didn't expect to be wearing him, but to have him close to me in any way at this point was oddly but perfectly acceptable to me. I imagined him laughing out loud about my lack of gracefulness, a quality those closest to me fully understand. But somehow I knew he approved, and he may have even helped the wind along because when he was alive, he was all about surprises. It was becoming more evident he was able to create surprises after his death, too.

The two memorial services in Kauai and Leysin were small gatherings with close friends and a more intimate sharing of heartfelt memories of Grant. The Charlevoix service was larger, with family, close friends, international business colleagues, and coworkers. Grant was a friend to everyone he met. He wasn't pretentious. He could drink top-shelf with a CEO or business partner in another country, or tell a joke and smoke a cigarette with someone he didn't know who was loading a truck at the docks. There was no shortage of people who had funny stories about him. Many shared ways he made them laugh, the lightness of his humor, and the ways he showed he cared about others. He knew how to make people feel special. It was his superpower. I missed this the most about him—how he made me feel special.

"STUPID SHIT" PEOPLE SAY AND DO

I wasn't prepared for the thoughtless or unusual things people say and do when you are grieving. I call these "stupid shit." I didn't have anyone to warn me about these more-than-likely unintentional, yet hurtful, things. Even if someone had cautioned me, I still don't think I could have expected or prepared myself for what happened at Grant's family memorial service in Flint, Michigan, where Grant was born and raised.

As I greeted and talked with people, many of whom I didn't know personally, I was often asked who I was and how I knew Grant. People seemed surprised when I said I was Grant's wife, responding with, "I'm so sorry for your loss" as if they had seen a ghost. Introducing yourself as the grieving widow at your husband's family hometown funeral is a fucking trip. Inevitably someone I didn't know would say something clueless about my husband, and I would stand there wondering why this person was attempting to talk to me. One woman said, "Maury, Grant's dad, is such a sweet man, but oh, of course your husband was even sweeter."

I said to her with a deadpan expression, "No, my husband wasn't really that sweet," and just walked away because I was exhausted from having meaningless conversations with people who didn't even know Grant or me. I know *they* were there for our family members because that is how you show you care. You show up to support people in some small way by being there. However, they—whoever *they* are—should have taken social etiquette classes about how to not say or do stupid shit at funerals and memorials. I'm not even sure if these classes exist, but they should!

Was this selfish of me? I don't know, but I decided I could be as selfish as I needed to be at this emotionally challenging time. I realized I needed to take care of myself and how I did that didn't need to make sense to anyone else. I figured if I couldn't be selfish about what I needed by protecting myself and my boundaries and occasionally telling someone to fuck off, then I probably wasn't taking care of myself as well as I should have.

My experience of what I call the *emotional grief wilderness*, a term I'm borrowing from death educator Dr. Alan Wolfelt, helped me to finally think about myself first for once and to put a hold on the people pleasing. I didn't have the energy to do it anymore. I found my voice, which was probably more passive-aggressive than it needed to be. I started to figure out more of what I was actually feeling, at least when I was sober. And finally, truth be told, I probably said "fuck off" under my breath more often than I ever did out loud.

As I made my way to be seated with Grant's immediate family at the funeral home, I realized that no one had put a chair for me next to all of them at the front of the room. *Seriously, what the fuck?!!!* My face flushed with surprise and embarrassment, especially because no one from Grant's immediate family noticed, and neither did the funeral director who was hosting the service and facing me. Did he see me standing there, the one who didn't have a chair? Uh, and I was the only one still standing! When no one paid attention to me, I looked around quickly to see where I could sit, and in that moment my gaze met Grant's best friend Darv, my anchor, who had an open seat next to him. I honestly didn't think I could feel more emotionally unhinged from my grief until that moment. I sat down and tried really hard to keep my shit together and not cry. I had to tell myself that it wasn't done maliciously. I was sure it was an honest mistake and maybe no one noticed. Especially if they didn't know who I was.

Later, at this same memorial, about an hour after lunch, Grant's cousin offered his condolences while he handed me a brown paper bag. I had no idea what was inside. He told me he had LSD, uppers, downers, and anything I might need. *Seriously, what the fuck?!* I asked his cousin, "What am I supposed to do with these?" The cousin told me to have a good time with my friends up north and cautioned me to not speed or get caught by the cops. Well, that was the last thing I needed! Did he think he knew me well enough to give me a bag of drugs? Maybe he and Grant had a different relationship than I knew about. I ended up taking the bag with me and offered it to friends who were happy to try new things. The only thing I wanted other than booze wasn't even in there, just some plain old Mary Jane.

What I began to realize is people give you what they think you need, because it is in fact what they need. Of course, they got it wrong because they weren't me. This reminds me of a quote I read once: "The first thing you should know about me is that I'm not you. A lot more will make sense after that." This should be the grievers' creed to live by.

CHANCE ENCOUNTER #1

A security guard from Wilcox Memorial Hospital on Kauai, where Grant had been in the ICU, was at Tradewinds bar one night when I was numbing my pain. He caught my eye and waved at me. Later, he came up to me to tell me how much he admired how I had cared for my husband during his stay in the hospital. I thanked him and made my way back to my car in the parking lot as quickly as I could, holding back my tears.

Once I locked myself in, I cried so hard I was shaking. How could something so innocent as an observer mentioning this set me off so dramatically? I didn't know, it just did. The experience in the ICU with Grant was one of the hardest emotional times of my life with him. He even told me to "Get the fuck out of my room" one day because he didn't want to see me after I showed up late. I was late because I was giving Grant's family an update on how he was doing, which was challenging with the Hawai'i-to-mainland time difference, which could be as much as six hours. I didn't know from one moment to the next if Grant was going to make it through his aspiration pneumonia. I felt helpless.

What I grew to realize is that the moment this gentleman approached me and in the most touching way shared his genuinely kind observation and sentiments, I began reliving that time in my life over again, like watching a painfully sad movie. But it wasn't a movie—it was my life.

GRANT GRIEF DREAM #1

My first dream about Grant was about a year after his death. He was in his wheelchair in the distance on Secret Beach with one of our caregivers. It was as if I was watching a movie of him taking in the beautiful day. I called his name and waved from a distance, but he couldn't see or hear me.

I felt awful that I couldn't have a positive experience of interacting with Grant in my dreams. It would be this way for years. I really wanted to dream about him. Ideally, I wanted him to take me on a worldly or perhaps even "other worldly" adventure. I've had about five dreams of Grant in total that I remember, and they were years apart, not happening as often as I would have liked. Why wasn't I dreaming about him more? Why wasn't he taking me on a grand adventure? I asked him about this, but never got an answer. All I could think is he must be really busy on the other side, but I preferred to think of him playing Frisbee on Secret Beach.

KEEPERS OF THE CRYSTAL

Grant had a best girl friend named Dana. He called her "Dana Machine," because she was always on the move. They grew up together as friends in middle school through high school, and were close until he died. I imagined that trouble found them as much as they looked for it. Dana, this beautiful being of light with painted fuchsia lips and green eyes as big as her smile, joined us through some of our most troubling times on our ALS journey. She wasn't afraid to be a part of the toughest times during our relationship. I was lucky she became one of my good friends, too, through many emotionally excruciating experiences. She was self-employed, then sold her food truck business and had some extra time and money to visit us in Kauai. She would stay with us for about two to four weeks at a time, her bright light of energy and humor a welcome break from the ordinary days.

After Grant died, Dana became my trusted confidante, growing closer as a friend to me. I think our connection kept that spark of Grant alive a little more for both of us. We called ourselves the "Keepers of the Crystal." Grant and Dana had a crystal they exchanged from a long time ago, before Grant met me. Each time they would see each other, the other one would get the crystal to keep until the next time. While Grant was ill, he asked me to have it made into a necklace for her. After we gave it to Dana, she kept it close to her heart.

On Dana's first visit after Grant's death, she told me the necklace had fallen onto the kitchen floor back in Florida where she lived. It shattered into several pieces. She was distraught and tried to glue it back together but knew it would never be the same. I wasn't at all surprised this had happened, because the crystal represented the connection between the two of them.

On another visit to Kauai, about a year after Grant's death, Dana stayed with me for about a month. Her visit overlapped with my Uncle Chris who was visiting from Johnston Atoll, where he worked as a chemical engineer. It was a relief to me that they had time to explore the island together while I was working at my friend's clothing store. But I was excited to enjoy a special evening out with two of my favorite people.

As my shift ended, I took the room charges to the front desk in the lobby, and when I returned my coworker said, "Hey, are you doing anything special tonight? Someone from a conference stopped in and said they had two people who couldn't attend. She wondered if someone would enjoy these two leis—there is one for a man and another for a woman." I hadn't yet told my coworker I had special dinner reservations at the Beach House Restaurant that night with Dana and my Uncle Chris. So I was especially in awe when I saw how beautiful and expensive these white ginger and sea grapes leis were, so delicately kept in their boxes. I told my coworker about my dinner plans. She was full of joy that she had accepted this unforeseen delivery, soon to be put to excellent use!

When I got home from work, I put the leis in the refrigerator and started to get ready. Dana came into my room and was fussing about her dress being too low cut and wondering if she should wear it, when I looked at her and said, "I've got the perfect thing to go with that!" I went downstairs to the fridge and pulled out the gorgeous white ginger lei. It had the most delicate fragrance and laid much like a lace collar around the neckline of her dress. I said "Aloha" while I placed the lei around her neck, letting it rest on her shoulders.

She beamed with the brightest smile and widest eyes ever and said, "Oh my gosh, Sheila, you didn't need to do this!" We were celebrating the 10-year anniversary of her sobriety and it was truly a special day. I confided in her, "I didn't do this…" and I told her the story of how they came to be that afternoon. She was in total shock and said, "Wow, I can't believe it. That Grantster is really something!" We truly believed he had somehow made this happen, because he was thoughtful like this in his human life. Grant would have absolutely done something special like this for Dana. The funny thing is that my Uncle Chris was sober for years, as well. It was a fine celebration with these two amazingly sober people. I couldn't wait to enjoy our evening.

As I drove to the Beach House on the South Shore, Dana talked about a lot of memories with Grant. She said, "I wonder what Grant would say about getting us these leis, if this happened when he was alive?" I told her I didn't know, but perhaps a waiter would say something very "Grant-like" and we would know by the end of our evening. After we enjoyed every bite of our delicious dinner, I drove home while thinking about Grant, and a very clear word popped into my head. I said, "Dana, do you know what Grant would say about all of this? 'Supercalifragilisticexpialidocious!'"

In the rear-view mirror, I could see her eyes light up and get big like saucers. She said, "Do you have any idea what that word means?!"

I said, "No, what does it…." and she interrupted me saying, "That is the word Grant used to make me say when we got high together in high school! We would laugh so hard because I could never say it with my dyslexia!" All I could think was, of course he was going to be a charismatic bright light from the other side, just as he was during his life. Why would he not be?

Also, he was getting really good at communicating with me!

INTO THE DEEP: FINAL EXIT

At one point during my caregiving journey with Grant, I came home from work and started cleaning up papers on the table of our front porch. I was surprised to find the book *Final Exit* at the bottom of the heap of newspapers. As I picked it up, I noticed the pages were dog-eared and highlighted in certain places. If someone had seen my face, the look of surprise and fear would have been hard to hide. I thought to myself, *Oh no, is Grant thinking about killing himself?*

At one point while we still lived in northern Michigan, Grant had said he might just float out to sea on an air cushion and decide to end it. Although I understood his physical and emotional pain, I didn't honestly think he would do it. Now that we were living in Kauai, this seemed like more of a possibility, and I started questioning whether he would. When we had a quiet moment together later that evening, I asked him about taking his own life. He said he and his friend were talking about it because he wanted to consider all of his options with the dreadful progression of this disease. I understood where he was coming from, even though I didn't want to think about this being a possibility.

After Grant died, Dana confided in me that he had talked to her about taking his life. He told her he would need help because, of course, he couldn't use his hands. She mulled this over while Grant struggled with his ALS. To my knowledge, the subject never came up between them again. I guessed he decided it was too painful to put this on his close friend. No matter how much she loved him, it would be hard for her. He never talked with me about any of these conversations. Dana told him she couldn't do it, as much as she loved him. She told me Grant respected her decision.

REFLECTION

After Grant's death, I knew I was a hot mess. On any given morning I might wake up and feel ashamed about something I had done at the bar the night before. This was the time of my life that I say I stumbled around a lot in the dark, looking for the light switch and my underwear. And not finding either—for years. The complicated emotions and intense grief brought me to my knees yet somehow, I was functioning in my day-to-day life, by making it to work like a normal human being, paying my bills, and showing up as a caring and loving friend.

I took care of my pets and loved ones who came to visit me, and overall functioned fine most of the time. I felt like I could cry at any moment, and there was often a bathroom nearby that I had staked out for the occasion. Working at the Marriott in its beautiful surroundings, with classic Hawaiian music playing in the background that I hear to this day in the back of my mind, took me away from my grief for a short while. I got to be on vacation with the tourists. I couldn't have been in a stressful job during this time, so in my world this was the perfect escape.

I think my ability to numb my emotions, through drinking, drugs, or medication, seriously messed up my natural ability to process my grief. Because over time, I discovered the only way to get through my grief was to emotionally go through it, to get to the other side. And that doesn't mean grief doesn't continue to visit me, like an unexpected and unwelcome guest. I truly believe there is no going around it, denying it, or pretending it doesn't exist. Because I've done all of that. And sometimes grief shows up unexpectedly, knocking the air out of you. I found that learning how to take better care of myself during the grief process was essential to my healing process.

The numbing of your emotions will eventually pummel you to the ground with yet another enveloping wave. You probably know by now that these "grief waves" are metaphors for grief-triggering experiences. I wish I knew how many of these rogue waves would inevitably hit me over the years, because they are a painful shock to the system. They come out from nowhere when you least expect them, triggered by something you could've never predicted in a million years. They bring you to your knees, and more often leave you gasping for breath. Your eyes and nose sting from the salt water, as you sit flat on your ass, with sand in places it shouldn't be, your swim bottoms floating to another island.

Self-Reflections

Below are some ways to navigate the roller coaster of complicated emotions and intense grieving.

Grounding yourself in the ability to be present in your own life can be the most challenging thing to do. Take the time to reflect upon this by going into the *Over the Rainbow Companion Journal*.

- ❀ Take an emotional inventory of all the feelings you are experiencing right now (see the Mood Scale/lists).

- ❀ Consider your emotional and mental process is a part of healing. Recognize what you have the choice and power to control and what you don't.

- ❀ Consider the idea that you must go through the emotional pain to get to the other side of it. How can you experience more of your feelings without judgment? Try to release your judgment and expectations of what you think this should look like.

- ❀ Review these stages from the Elisabeth Kübler-Ross' and other grief experts including Seven Stages Model of Grief and see where you are today:

- Shock and denial—emotionally numb
- Pain and guilt
- Anger and bargaining
- Depression and loneliness
- The Upward Turn—calmer with some adjustment
- Reconstruction and working through the feelings
- Acceptance and hope

❀ Nurturing yourself through this process is the key—and often the hardest part. When you numb yourself with whatever "methods" are available to you—alcohol, drugs, food, social media, Netflix bingeing—you defeat this purpose. While it is good to take "grief breaks," these coping methods don't actually help you through your process.

❀ Remember there is no specific timetable and, in fact, time does not necessarily heal all wounds. It diminishes memory or in some cases might make it stronger.

❀ Write about your feelings in your *Over the Rainbow Companion Journal*. There is a place where you can share more about your personal grief story.

❀ Self-soothe when you're hurting: Use your five senses—visually review photos you have of your loved ones; listen to music or guided meditations before bed with your playlist of favorite songs; pet your loving animal or something soft, or use a weighted blanket; light a candle or fill a diffuser with your favorite scent; eat a warm dessert or comfort food, drink tea, coffee, or a favorite beverage, or infuse water with berries, mint, cucumber, etc.

CHAPTER PLAYLIST/GUIDED MEDITATIONS

- "I Will Remember You," Sarah McLachlan
- "Angel," Sarah McLachlan
- "Into the Mystic," Van Morrison
- For guided meditations, visit SheilaClemenson.com.

RESOURCES

- *365 Days of Understanding Your Grief: Daily Readings for Finding Hope and Healing Your Heart,* Alan D. Wolfelt, Ph.D.
- *Grief One Day at a Time: 365 Meditations to Help You Heal After Loss,* Alan D. Wolfelt, Ph.D.
- *Understanding Your Grief: Ten Essential Touchstones for Finding Hope and Healing in Your Heart,* Alan D. Wolfelt, Ph.D.
- *The Wilderness of Grief: Finding Your Way,* Alan D. Wolfelt, Ph.D.

CHAPTER 3
It Takes an Island

> "We are like islands in the sea, separate on the surface but connected in the deep."
>
> — *William James*

THE WAITING GAME

How did Grant and I wake up each day and move forward? Making it through this experience seemed impossible. And I was painfully aware that we wouldn't make it through together. How does one accept this and continue to move on each day?

Some days were better than others. And I prayed for good days. Blessed and grateful for the kindness of friends, family, and strangers. I prayed to God every morning that we would have a stronger day with more lighthearted moments, less pain, greater strength and mobility, more smiles, less anger, and fewer tears. All of this was brutally hard. Waiting for my beloved to die was the ultimate test in maintaining my sanity and patience. It is the hardest experience to describe, but if you've been through it, then you know. You don't want your loved one to die. And you don't know how much longer you can physically and emotionally endure the pain of losing that person while they are still alive. There is so much guilt when you think about how much easier your life will be without your loved one. It still doesn't mean you would choose that option. But I can't honestly say that I didn't fantasize once in a while about running away from home. In the later stages of ALS, Grant didn't want to die, but he certainly didn't want to live and suffer any longer. This illness was the most grueling experience one can imagine. I was most likely going to survive it. But it was hard to imagine how much more painful the experience was going to be without him.

PATIENCE

If you've been a caregiver, you might know something about patience. Patiently waiting for your loved one to do anything—in this particular situation waiting for Grant to drink a smoothie for breakfast—was challenging for him physically and hard for me emotionally to watch him struggle. It was hard for him to swallow, and he needed to take his time so he wouldn't choke and aspirate while drinking it. We tried to get him as many daily calories as we could in the last six months of his life.

Going to the bathroom was another challenging situation. Once I got over the mental block of wiping my beloved's ass, and then Grant got over me actually doing it, we moved into a more routine place with this.

One day, while I helped Grant go to the bathroom, I held his head up with the palm of my hand as he sat on the toilet. He said, "So when we first met, did you ever think we would be doing this together?" We both laughed. Grant always had a way of making awkward situations more bearable. His ability to express himself with a wicked sense of humor that was larger than life is one of the things I loved most about him. And he loved making others laugh. In our situation, if you weren't laughing, you were crying from all of the stress. Physically taking care of someone with full caregiving needs—total activities of daily living—day in and day out was wearing me out. I have never run a marathon, so I can't speak from personal experience, but I was a runner in my younger years, and I felt like I was running through several marathons strung together. It was that level of pure exhaustion. As a sprinter, I was in my final quarter of the mile relay race, completely strung out in mental exhaustion, as well.

TUESDAYS WITH MORRIE

Tuesdays with Morrie is a book by Mitch Albom, whom I knew as a sports columnist with the *Detroit Free Press*, as I'm a Michigander. Mitch wrote about his professor, Morrie, who was living with ALS, the same disease that Grant had. Published in 1997, it was many readers' first introduction to this devastating illness that would gradually take away Grant's self-expression and eventually his life.

I read the book shortly after I heard of it, about two years after Grant was diagnosed with ALS. Although the book was a profound inspiration to many, it actually made me angry. I needed to ask myself why I felt this way. I thought about the conversations between Morrie and Mitch, and the special times they had together. And then it hit me, as I read the cover blurb: "an old man, a young man, and life's greatest lessons." Morrie was a dying old man who had lived a long, meaningful, and rich life. Grant and I had been cheated out of our long life together. As I thought more about it, it rubbed me even more raw, just as raw as I had scratched my irritated skin until it bled. I found myself wondering, *Where was Morrie's wife when all of these meetings were happening on Tuesdays? Did she ever take these meetings as an opportunity to run away from home?* Because this is what I felt like doing on so many of our bad days together. I knew one thing, we were not as conscious and spiritually evolved as Morrie, sharing his life's lessons with Mitch.

Why was I living in this shit storm? On any given day, why was I stepping around this shit?

This "shit" was my term for our painful human emotional experience and fallout as a result of living through this illness. I was not as highly evolved as Morrie, but a more emotionally flawed human going through the most painful experience I might ever imagine—at 29 years old. Every day I felt as if I was walking in a field of landmines, dreading an explosion underfoot.

I had become a safe place for Grant's temper and unrealistic expectations to explode. As his illness progressed, I felt like his caregiver first and his wife second. I felt like I let him down on a daily basis and it was hard to live with this. People might say, "Don't sweat the small stuff," or my favorite, "Let that shit go," but in real life it is so much easier to say and an impossible feat to actually do.

DIRTY LAUNDRY

It wasn't easy letting other people see all of our "dirty laundry"—literally, yes, but over time more figuratively, too. It was difficult to manage our boundaries when we needed other people to come into our lives and help with all of the day-to-day responsibilities and duties that were becoming so incredibly hard for me to do on my own. We still wanted our privacy and our personal needs taken care of in our own way. It was a huge lesson in letting go and surrendering, otherwise I would be completely burned out.

Standing up for myself and my needs was stressful. It was often easier to just listen to Grant yell at me, apologize for something I wasn't truly sorry for, and then move on with the rest of the day. It is hard to be your best on little to no sleep, feeling cranky, tired, or unforgiving in the moment for even the slightest error in judgment or a harsh word yelled in frustration.

We knew how to press each other's buttons and eventually did it in front of others, without thinking much about it. This behavior became a vicious cycle from which we couldn't break free. I know we were relieved when help was on the way, hopeful to get a break from each other. Grant and I held high expectations of ourselves and one another. Sometimes he would reprimand me in a condescending manner for not "having it all together." However, he would go easy on me at other times, and sometimes I was the one being hard on myself. Accepting help from others was difficult for both of us. Visiting guests could be really good at reading our minds, which was such a relief. Whether they did or not, though, their support, love, and understanding was a pure blessing.

SÃO PAULO AND RIO DE JANEIRO

There wasn't much I wouldn't do for Grant. I loved him more than life itself. When he told me he wanted to go see friends in São Paulo, Brazil, in a fragile physical state and getting worse, I thought he was insane.

This was six months before he died. Grant had a much harder time holding up his head on his own but refused to wear a neck brace much of the time. His energy was waning, and he did not have much stamina. Grant talked with his good friend, Tim, and we discovered he was on board for the adventure to South America.

I was hanging on by a thread of sanity and it showed. The stress I was under, traveling with Grant from Kauai to Miami and then on to São Paulo, was beyond intense. It was hard for our Brazilian friends to understand the concept of preserving Grant's energy, especially because he did his best to hide how tired he was. By the end of the day, he was exhausted, a little drunk, and a difficult patient. Our caregiving routine was a crucial and necessary structure in our lives, and that was thrown to hell in a handbasket on this trip. I felt like I was an ungrateful guest of Grant's business colleagues' hospitality; however, my stress was off the charts. At this point, I was consumed by his daily living physical needs. I was emotionally burned out, physically exhausted, and on my last nerve without much patience at all.

Despite all of this, we took a side trip to Rio de Janeiro for a couple of days. One of our highlights was seeing Christ the Redeemer, a sacred landmark for the city. Our friends found a couple of generous souls, and for the right price, they carried Grant to the top in his wheelchair. People were able to make things happen for Grant and I was along for the ride, not ungrateful to have the experience and trying to make the best of it. But I seriously doubted our marriage was going to survive this trip. In fact, before we returned home, he told me he was considering divorcing me. I told him if he had the energy to do so, to go for it.

When we returned home, I ended up coordinating five caregivers to care for him for about two weeks so we could have desperately needed time apart. I went back to Michigan to see my family. When I came back, we greeted each other with tears in our eyes, professing our love for one another. And then I took Grant to the emergency room that evening with aspiration pneumonia. This became the beginning of the end of his life, as noted in our Secret Beach story.

OUR SOUL CONTRACT

I constantly questioned my purpose while on my caregiving journey with Grant. I had a strong belief in God/Goddess/Great Spirit. I believed in the power of prayer and positive thinking. Some days I needed to be strong enough for both of us. I was open to all types of healing modalities and constantly researched new developments about ALS. We needed to weigh the pros and cons of many healing modalities, especially because of the money factor. I would share my findings with Grant and often he wouldn't give me his full attention, being otherwise engaged in something or not really listening to me at all.

I figured this was the stage of denial that Elisabeth Kübler-Ross shares about in her book *On Death and Dying*.

Not a day passed that I didn't wonder why this was happening to such a vibrant, funny, and charismatic soul. I wanted a long life with him more than anything. I was always searching for answers, no matter how outlandish or unconventional. One afternoon in my home on Kauai, a friend who was visiting referred me to a spiritual intuitive, also known as a psychic, whom she trusted. Our friend told me this psychic had shared many things he could never know. I decided to schedule a phone session with him.

In the first words out of this psychic's mouth, he told me that Grant and I had made a soul contract with one another before we came to Earth for this incarnation. This has to do with belief in reincarnation, that we come here in many different lives throughout time and space. I was open-minded and found this idea intriguing. I wanted to know more.

He said my role was to love Grant unconditionally as his wife and caregiver, and this would help Grant to heal his soul wound, to be loved in this way in this lifetime. Grant's role was to help me heal my fears of abandonment by loving me with all of his heart, to help me heal from the fears I held in this and other lifetimes.

I had never mentioned to the psychic that my dad died by suicide when I was 5 years old. But the psychic repeated, "By Grant leaving you from this loving place in his heart, you will be healed of this deep soul wound. You are doing the same for him in his need to feel and experience unconditional love in this lifetime."

I didn't share much about us in advance of meeting with this psychic. But I didn't care if anyone had told him about us. The information he shared was a healing balm for my heart and soul. Suddenly, everything resonated and made sense. I was blown away.

While Grant was sick, I questioned my purpose in supporting him through his illness. My belief in God/Goddess/Great Spirit and healing was strong enough for both of us, though, and perhaps at times it needed to be. I came to realize in the depths of my heart and soul that when you ask the Great Spirit for support and answers, you need to be open to responses coming to light in different and unexpected ways. I learned and trusted these answers to come with time.

Different types of healing modalities came into my experience in different ways. I presented them to Grant on a regular basis, as if I was some kind of conduit. Sometimes he would engage in them, such as the acupuncture and energy medicine work he did weekly with a well-respected practitioner in Kauai. He would have regular weekly massages and physical therapy, and we were accepted into a drug study for which I needed to give Grant two injections per day.

The most unusual thing he agreed to do, earlier in his diagnosis, was a Benny Hinn Christian Miracle Crusade. Benny Hinn is a televangelist, best known for his faith healing summits held in stadiums in major cities. He is a controversial faith healer who teaches about a power given by God through him to carry out healings of illnesses such as blindness, deafness, cancer, AIDS, and severe physical injuries. I dragged Grant to Seattle. Grant said he'd always wanted to see the city and that is why I think he entertained the idea, plus he had a favorite aunt we needed to visit.

Other times, Grant said he wanted nothing to do with my suggestions, like the hands-on healer Dean Kraft. I actually talked to a client of Dean Kraft whom he healed of ALS. I pursued this healing experience and found out we would have needed to move to Manhattan, New York to work with this hands-on healer. Once I shared this with Grant, he told me there was no way he was moving from Kauai. He was adamant about that. Ultimately, I would present ideas and thoughts about what we could do to support his healing. I trusted Grant to make his own decisions, but it was hard for me to not want to insist on some things, only because I didn't want to lose him. I did recognize there were those who take advantage of people in our situation. We had our eyes and hearts wide open, though. We prayed for a miracle, while preparing for the worst.

UNCONDITIONAL LOVE

Grant sat in his recliner while I placed his hands and feet in a more comfortable position. As I did this, he looked me straight in the eyes and said, "I think you bit off more than you can chew."

I thoughtfully replied, "Well, yes, but I'm still here, wiping your ass, and I'm not going anywhere."

I didn't add what I was thinking, *All of this despite you trying to continuously push me away.* This was about three years into our marathon nightmare with ALS.

As I got Grant settled into his chair with a TV remote while he waited for his caregiver to arrive, I figured that I must have looked more frazzled than usual. Just because I had already accepted that he was attempting to push me away didn't make it any easier to deal with on a day-to-day basis. Grant could have a razor sharp tongue and verbally discipline me when I didn't properly anticipate his needs. He would say, "You should know what I need by now." The hard part was his needs changed drastically about every two months. He lost the ability to do more with each passing month. I knew both of us were living in some kind of denial. Not that it was happening, but perhaps that it was happening faster than we thought it would or that he was losing the ability to do much for himself anymore.

Our intimacy was compromised because of his all-consuming needs and my growing resentment. Once his caregiver arrived, whoever it was, he would be as sweet as pie, saying to them, "How did you sleep last night, honey? You look tired and like you need a nap." The funny, or I guess not so funny, thing is that he never noticed this about me. If I could do it all over, I would have invested more of our retirement money in caregivers so that I could be Grant's wife. I do think I bit off more than I could chew. And with each passing day, his illness took over more of his funny, charming lightness, of being "The Grantster," the man I fell in love with. He was quite a bit of his dad, Pappy, but also like his mom, too.

Grant's mom, Caroline, had died of pancreatic cancer a couple of years before we met. I never had the opportunity to know her, but I heard stories about her. Pappy would tell me, "Carol was the best-dressed woman in Flint, Michigan." This was the polite way he described her shopping obsession: she decided to buy two pairs of the same shoes just to spite him because he had told her he would give her money for both pairs if she didn't buy them. After Carol died, the family found many tags on clothes she had never worn, and jewelry in boxes stashed in odd places around the house. She struck me as an emotional woman with an edgy side to her personality. I could see how Grant took after her a bit in some ways, or maybe more as he became an out-of-control "control freak." There were countless things he had no control over, and the list grew consistently. It was a different level of insanity in my already challenged world. I imagine Grant telling me that I'm not perfect either, and he is absolutely right. He would appreciate that I admit this, after talking shit about him when he can't defend himself now that he's dead. I know I drove him as crazy as he drove me nuts. I think that's about right.

SEVEN SACRED POOLS

Sometime after Grant died, I was going through his things and found black sand he had collected in a plastic film canister from Hana on Maui when we visited the Seven Sacred Pools in 1995, the same trip when we got engaged. At the time, I questioned whether he should have been collecting it. But he brought it back home to Petoskey in 1995, then transported it with our move out to Kauai in 1997. I was aware of the warnings about taking lava rocks and black sand from the islands. This is called "The Curse of Pele."

Pele, the goddess of fire, is known for her temper. According to legend, Pele is so angered when rocks are taken from her that she exacts a terrible revenge on the thief. It is said this curse was created by a park ranger in the 1940s who wanted to stop tourists from taking sacred lava rocks from the island of Hawai'i. Locals and tourists alike think it may have been Pele herself who created this curse, due to the stories of bad luck and trauma shared in letters and various stories in the news, travel sites, and blogs. The Visitor Center of Hawai'i's Volcanoes National Park has received thousands of letters, many with lava rocks or black sand returned over the years by tourists who have taken them as souvenirs from the islands.

I didn't believe in this curse at the time, but I wasn't about to test it either. I figured Grant had been coming to the islands long before knowing the proper Hawaiian customs and traditions. To be clear, Grant had symptoms and was seeing medical specialists before we went to Hawaii on our first trip together to Kauai and Maui in April 1995. However, his ALS diagnosis came three months after we returned to Petoskey, in July 1995. I've thought about this curse from time to time. Although I'm not sure I believe in it, I finally returned the black sand to the island of Maui when I was there in 2005, working on my "shitty first book." You'll read about this in an upcoming chapter.

KAUAI WELLNESS RETREAT CLASSES

Early in our life on Kauai, we learned about Wellness Retreat Classes at Kauai Community College including art therapy, Reiki, and group therapy sessions. This is where I met my counseling therapist, Reenie. I called her from home one day, overwrought with frustration and dangling by a thread. I needed to schedule an appointment to see her, or I was planning to check myself into Mahelona Psychiatric Hospital down the street from where we lived in Kapahi. Some people say God doesn't give you more than you can handle. Well, I question the existence of mental institutions and prisons. And I beg to differ on that one.

Just one conversation with Reenie, and I suddenly felt like I had met the nurturing person that I always needed through this experience. Reenie looked very much like, but was a softer version of, Bea Arthur, from *Maude* and *The*

Golden Girls. She said something profound to me before we hung up. She said, "You can make it through this successfully." I never thought that was an option. The fact she planted that possibility helped me more than I ever imagined. I was fighting to hold my shit together with each passing day as mine and Grant's arguments got worse. He said he didn't need a therapist, but he thought I very much did, so I should go. It was the best thing I could have ever done for myself. I believe I wouldn't have made it through the end of Grant's illness and through my grieving process without her. I think everyone needs to find their own Reenie.

INTO THE DEEP: SUICIDE

Warning to reader: This section is about family tragedy, suicide, and physical abuse.

I was 5 years old when my dad took his own life at 23 years old, the result of depression and not having the coping skills to deal with the unraveling of his life and marriage to my mom. Due to my age, my mom, also 23 years old, told me he died in a car accident. I know my mom was trying to protect me. Would a 5-year-old understand her dad died from suicide? Probably not. However, I wish this difficult conversation had happened when I was old enough to understand the concept of suicide. I'm aware that life with a teenager doesn't easily allow conversations about doing the dishes, much less something of this tragic and devastating nature. Suicide was very much a taboo subject in June 1973 when it happened, and it still is today.

My aunt eventually told me when I was around 15 years old what really happened when my dad died. It was on an evening when she stayed overnight—my mom was already in bed, and as night owls, we stayed up late talking while she finished a large tumbler of scotch with cigarettes. I was probably complaining about how much better my life would be if my real dad was still alive. I guess she thought it was time I knew the truth. It wasn't unusual for us to have deep conversations together. We were very close through many difficult times in my life.

I wondered if my family had more dark secrets than other families. This thought was immediately confirmed when my aunt shared on this same occasion a traumatic story about my mom being physically abused by my dad. She told me my mom woke up in the middle of the night with my dad's fist in her face. I said, "Holy shit! How the hell did my mom survive this? What kind of hell has she been through?"

My aunt shared how she physically cared for my mom and me during that awful time of physical abuse, then later after my dad died. Knowing this made me concerned about my mom. She had been through a lot. Of course, the truth shattered all of my idealistic memories of my dad. I had idolized him! Before I knew the truth, I'd thought often about how much more perfect and wonderful my life would be if my dad were still alive. I was a hormonal teenager going through extremely challenging times (I'll share more in the next chapter).

All of this was devastating for me to hear. Thinking back, I actually remember seeing bloody washcloths in the bathroom. I'm not sure what my younger self thought. Could it have been from a bloody nose or cutting yourself shaving? Would I have thought that at that age? I don't remember anything else. My mom assured me that I was never physically abused by my dad. We finally talked about it in my twenties. At that time, my mom finally told me my dad killed himself on the day he was scheduled to meet her at the attorney's office to file for divorce. She was waiting for him, and he never showed up.

Wow, how do you deal with that? I asked her, "Mom, how the hell did you survive all of this?" and she said, "Well, I needed to take care of you."

This was my mom's love for me: armoring up to do what she needed to do. I had a newfound sense of respect and compassion for her painful journey.

My father's death set the underlying foundation for all of my abandonment issues. Grant's death was another devastating opportunity to work through it once again.

REFLECTION

If you ask me what I'm most proud of in my life, it is walking the journey of ALS with Grant. I'm proud that I was able to be there with him through the good, sweetness of life and then through the challenging struggles and pain. This is one of my greatest accomplishments in this particular life. However, I know I couldn't have done this without the help of so many. Grant's dad, Pappy, would say to me whenever I saw him, "We know Grant would have never had the beautiful life he wanted at the end without you. We're so grateful he had you. I don't know what we would have done without you." And I don't know what I would have done without my family and friends.

Which brings us to the adult role in grief, taking care of your kids and other people who need you. The world doesn't stop when someone dies the way most people would like it to.

How can you show up as a caregiver for yourself and others in your life? How do you minimize your own feelings and experiences to your own detriment or burden?

I've grown to trust the answers will come in time, but I do need to ask for them. I feel a soulful bond with Grant and imagine he is one of my guardian angels. He helps me from the other side and is there when I need him. I know this with my full being. I believe the power of the Great Spirit and the Universe is beyond human comprehension. We need to be willing to surrender our need to be in control. This is when the real magic happens.

At some point early in my grief, I found a greeting card with a black and white photo of a young girl, about three years old, standing in the rain with her hands up in the air to feel the rain falling down. On it was written, "Then when it seems we will never smile again, life comes back…" I bought this card when I was heavily grieving so many years ago, to remind myself that I would get to this place within me again. Now, it reminds me of where I was in those dark times and that, yes, I know with all of my heart and soul that if you work hard on your personal grief, life does come back, and you will smile again.

Self-Reflection

Become a more conscious caregiver of yourself and others.

What does this look like if you are a people pleaser and put the needs of others before your own? This can be for both physical and emotional needs, especially if you have children you are supporting through this grief process, too. Go to the *Over the Rainbow Companion Journal* for the following:

1. Identify that your needs come first, and then you need to decide how you will share and communicate about them.

    - Substitute the acronym of FEAR—false evidence appearing real—with a new one:
    - Face your fear,
    - Evaluate the evidence,
    - Analyze what is true, and
    - Reframe what is happening for you.

2. What is the most important thing you need to do today? Take small bites of the elephant.

3. If you are feeling overwhelmed, who can you invite in to help you?

4. Explore your personal values and boundaries. Take the inventory in your *Over the Rainbow Companion Journal*.

5. What makes up your spiritual garden? Your spiritual garden is a place where nature is celebrated, and it includes anything that physically brings you an atmosphere of peace and connection. This can be an actual place, an altar in your home or outside, or one you create in your mind during meditation. A deeper spiritual meaning is your relationship with a higher power, God, the Divine, Great Spirit, or the Universe. What is just for you that you don't need to share with other people?

Here are suggestions to help you manage negative, difficult, and draining emotions:

1. Honor all of your feelings and get more familiar with what they are called. Explore Dr. Brené Brown's book *Atlas of the Heart: Mapping Meaningful Connection and the Language of Human Experience*. In it, Brown shares, "I want this book to be an atlas for all of us, because I believe that, with an adventurous heart and the right maps, we can travel anywhere and never fear losing ourselves."

2. Limit your social media consumption.

3. Make time to "feel your feelings," giving yourself time and space to process them, without judgment or needing to do anything about them.

4. Write in a journal. Put your feelings into words and use the *Over the Rainbow Companion Journa*l to support your process. Share it with a friend, therapist, or grief support group.

5. Check out VeryWellMind.com and the VeryWell Mind podcast with Amy Morin, LCSW.

6. Visit davidkesslertraining.com/tenderhearts, which is a grief support community with grief expert David Kessler.

7. You need support, but you don't know what to do or where to start? Contact your most resourceful family member or friend and ask them to help you figure out what you need to do. It is hard to ask for help, but sometimes you need to take the first step.

CHAPTER PLAYLIST/GUIDED MEDITATIONS

- "Tears in Heaven," Eric Clapton, with songwriter Will Jennings
- "Lift Me Up," Rhianna, from *Black Panther: Wakanda Forever*, as a tribute to the late actor Chadwick Boseman
- For guided meditations, visit SheilaClemenson.com.

RESOURCES

- *The Caregiver's Companion: Words to Comfort and Inspire*, Betty Clare Moffatt
- *Companioning the Bereaved: A Soulful Guide for Caregivers*, Alan D. Wolfelt, Ph.D.
- The Working Daughter, a Facebook Group
- Recommended reading by Mitch Albom:
  - *Tuesdays With Morrie: an Old Man, a Young Man, and Life's Greatest Lesson*
  - *The Five People You Meet in Heaven*, *The First Phone Call from Heaven*, *For One More Day*
  - *Have a Little Faith*
  - *The Time Keeper*
- Relevant healing professional publications:
  - *Ask the Body and Treat the Priority*, Molly Jones, L.Ac.—Acupuncturist and Vibrational Medicine
  - *A Touch of Hope: The Autobiography of a Laying-on-of-Hands Healer*, Dean and Rochelle Kraft

CHAPTER 4
The Life Jacket: Self-Love and Worthiness

"Dance with the waves, move with the sea, let the
rhythm of the water set your soul free."

— *Christy Ann Martine*

CONFESSIONS OF A GRIEVING YOUNG WIDOW

For the first few years, I was properly medicated and numbing myself with alcohol. More often than I would like to admit, I picked up strangers, good-looking men I had met in a bar or nightclub. I told myself I was having fun. I needed to feel good, attractive, and alive, but more importantly that I deserved to have a good time. I would walk into a bar and say to a friend or just to myself, "I'm going to take him home tonight." And then, I would do just that. The bar was my playground. Sometimes I dated someone for a few weeks if they were locally based, and other times they were single vacationers with no opportunities for commitment. I thought I was done with committed relationships. Sometimes I would remember their names and if I ran into one of them today, I might call him a friend. But one thing is for sure. I will always remember the circumstances around why it would have never worked out between us.

Looking puzzled, some people ask me why I left Kauai, a beautiful tropical paradise. I jokingly say, "I dated all of the single men, available and maybe not so available, on the island." But I wasn't joking, and I eventually discovered I was the one who wasn't emotionally available. And just like a mirror, that is who I attracted, the emotionally unavailable guy. They might show up as the *hapa* local guy, the short radio D.J., the real estate agent, the golfing buddy, the waiter, the bass player, the flight attendant, the executive chef, and then more seriously, well over a year after Grant had died, the physical therapist who became my longest relationship on and off the island. That's when I found out how unavailable I really was.

At the end of this especially close relationship, my heart ached with longing because I had fallen in love with him. When he moved away from the island, I found out how much more healing work on myself I needed to do. I didn't see this at the time, but what I needed was to love myself. We continued a long-distance international relationship over the next couple of years, one I would put in the category of "friends with benefits" when we met on vacations together. He was exactly the relationship I needed at that time in my life. And although I thought I wanted more, I guess I was lucky in hindsight that he wasn't the marrying type. But he broke my heart, and this was just another layer of loss for me to move through.

SHE JUST WANTS TO DANCE

To dance with reckless abandon, my hair swirling aimlessly with my head rocking out to the music, was always a wonderful way for me to release stress and to play. From high school dances after football games in the '80s to nightclubs in my twenties, I always had fun dancing with others. People who know me well might call me a party waiting to happen, so I think the "party girl" is one of my personas. When I met Grant, we danced a lot together. He would jump up, clap his hands, and then go down on his hands and knees and yell, "Surf on my back!" usually to the B-52s "Rock Lobster" song. It was zany fun, and of course, I played along. We loved dancing together and I missed that joy greatly during his illness and after his death.

One night my roommate Holly, the same Holly who was Grant's caregiver, asked me if I wanted to go out dancing. I was getting cozy with a box of Kleenex and putting on the movie *City of Angels* with Meg Ryan and Nick Cage, a real tearjerker. Her question made me think, and I froze with indecision.

Holly was dating several people at this time, and I didn't expect her to come home and ask me to go out. Was I really in the mood to go out dancing? I started crying because I didn't know what I wanted to do. She looked at me and in a gentle voice said, "It's OK if you want to stay home and cry your eyes out; that's fine. Or you can decide to go out with me and have a good time. It's up to you."

I wasn't one to stay home alone and drink, because I was the party girl. And yes, I did think I could rally, put my face on, and that it might do me some good. The thing about going out when I rallied, though, was I just might decide to pick up someone from the bar and go home with him. This could include bringing him back to our place or going to someone's hotel room. On this particular night, I decided to pick up a cute guy who happened to be a flight attendant on an overnight stay. I didn't normally remember too many details about what happened on these nights and this occasion was no different. It was kind of like playing Russian roulette: I was gambling with an STD or the chance of going home with a psycho. At the time I didn't really care. Maybe I had a death wish and was testing fate. I truly believe my guardian angels were on overdrive because time and again, fortunately I was with good guys who didn't take advantage of me, rape, or kill me. Sometimes I saw them again, planned to see them again, but never did or whatever. I guess this depended on how good of a time I thought I had and if he ever called again.

I didn't think I was attached to any of these men until I was feeling the excitement of a new relationship. Then I wanted to see them again or I was infatuated and wanted to marry them. All I can say is that I had physical needs that seemed to be insatiable, especially when I was drinking. I had no discernment or much control of my reckless behavior when under the influence. With the alcoholic genes on both sides of my family, I pushed the boundaries. I think deep down I knew perfectly well what I was doing and in fact had it mapped out in my mind when I connected with just the right unavailable guy who was either visiting or living on the island.

I will never forget a short time before Grant died, he was lying in bed and started to cry. I asked him what was going on. He confided his fears of not being able to take care of me anymore. He said, "You were really into dating guys who didn't treat you well when I first met you, and somehow I know you're going back to that place, and I won't be able to protect you anymore."

I tried to assure him that I had changed and that I was going to be OK, but he knew me well.

THOUGHT DISTORTIONS

I lied to myself in many ways. At times this was denial or, more positively, wishful thinking. I lost myself in caring for Grant's needs for so many years, I didn't know what I needed anymore. In fact, I didn't even know where to start. It was like the floodgates opened and from this place in my reality, my needs, mostly emotional and physical—the needs to be loved, nurtured, and comforted—were acted out in desperation.

I needed physical touch but didn't know at the time it was my number one love language. I wanted desperately to get out of this dark, lonely place and to feel loved, needed, and wanted again. Social drinking, partying, and having sexual relationships were my ways of filling this void. And they were never going to fill my love tank. I didn't know how to love myself or to be my own best friend. I had no idea what true self-care looked like because I was trying to be filled by everything else outside of me. Truthfully, I was running away from myself because it hurt too much to sit with all of my inner feelings and pain.

Why couldn't I see this? Why couldn't I see my own light? Why couldn't I find the beauty of the days when I was vibrant and healthy, the way I was when I was so deeply in love with Grant? Sometimes I felt so very alone. I needed to take care of myself, but more importantly I needed to love myself in a way no other person could.

GRANT GRIEF DREAM #2

In the second dream I had about Grant, he was talking on the phone while working in his home office. He sat at his desk, and while I walked toward the door to greet him, he stood up and walked to the door on his side, gesturing "Shhh" with his finger to his lips for me to be quiet. Then he closed the door in my face.

When I woke up, I was so upset. Why would he close the door in my face? I couldn't figure out why he couldn't or wouldn't talk to me! I was so distraught. I can only imagine that for some reason he couldn't interact with me from the other side or something like that. I didn't know if he was limited on visitations during my sleeping hours or what. I just knew I wanted to be with him, as we were in better times when he was healthy. I had the sense he was trying to connect with me, but at the same time he couldn't communicate with me. He made this crystal clear by shutting the door in my face.

This kind of dream was a really hard start to my day. I needed to move through the emotions of it, typically before showing up for work, and needing to be in a good mood with my smile on.

WHAT I NEEDED

I knew I needed to manage my grief around people, places, and things. I did this in a less planned, but more organic way during Grant's illness while living in anticipatory grief, and then more fully during my bereavement after Grant's death. I stayed away from people I didn't feel supported by. I avoided situations I thought might trigger me, and realized I was sensitive about things that reminded me of Grant. They could be what we'd done together, whether in the distant or more recent past, or places where we had some of our last experiences together. Most evident was the low setting on my bullshit meter.

I had a low tolerance for people who complained about irrelevant shit. I didn't have time for petty nonsense, like people treating me poorly or being disrespectful. I found comfort in being around people who knew me and knew what I had been through. It was harder for me to connect with people who didn't know what great loss was about and those who hadn't experienced a substantial death in their life. I needed to be with people whose presence made me feel safe. Though it was interesting that when I was drinking, none of this mattered as much.

I loved going to the beach, walking it or taking a nap there where I could hear the crashing ocean waves in the distance. I needed the beach and ocean air. I needed to be surrounded by my *ohana* who I knew loved me. I didn't think I needed much on the small island of Kauai: flip-flops called "slippahs," a sarong, a bathing suit, and the best *ohana* this *wahine* was lucky to find. My life was moving into a better place in my grief. There were moments of happiness, laughter, and joy. I could feel the sun on my face on more days while standing at the edge of the grief pit.

THE LIFE JACKET: SELF-LOVE AND WORTHINESS

INTO THE DEEP: SEXUAL ABUSE

Warning: This section is about childhood sexual abuse.

I understood, through Grant's experience and from those deep emotional experiences of my past, that I didn't want to depend upon another person for my daily existence or survival.

Heartfelt, empathetic, loving, and nurturing are words that describe me, but I didn't always feel this way as a caregiver. I felt resentful and challenged, and it was sometimes very hard for me to be understanding even though Grant was enduring the worst human experience possible with his ALS.

I grieved with him for our losses—his and mine. I understood what it was like to be disabled and limited because I lived through the entire experience with Grant as he grew weaker and could no longer use his arms, hands, and legs. I knew what it meant to be dependent upon another human being for everything, because I became that person for Grant. In addition, six years older than me, he was my financial anchor, as a successful businessman who had invested and created the opportunity to afford taking an "early retirement" to live on Kauai. Financially, we were lucky to move there five years after Hurricane Iniki, a Category 5 storm which tragically devastated the island in 1992. The locals were rebuilding at the time, and we were fortunate to rent a three-bedroom, two bath, smaller home for $500 per month.

While Grant could be generous with his money, he could also be controlling about the financial purse strings. This would trigger me from time to time and remind me of what I had experienced at a younger age.

When I was 8 years old, my mom remarried and suddenly I had a stepfather. It was strange to call him "Dad," but I was so happy to have a dad in my life. He was always nice to me, especially while they were dating. He liked to tell jokes and, overall, he had a happy-go-lucky nature. We did a lot of fun things together as a family, including beach vacations and camping.

When I was about 10, he started asking me to let him rub up against me while I was lying on the floor watching TV or doing homework after school when my mom was still working. Sometimes it was with his clothes on and then eventually, it was without anything under his bathrobe. If I wanted to go play with my friends, wanted new clothes, or to go to the mall, essentially anything that a pre-teen girl would love to do or have, then I needed to let him do this to me.

My mom was working full-time and going to nursing school in an effort to get a better-paying job. All the while, my stepfather spent a lot of money that we didn't have on things for himself he didn't really need. The Social Security I received when my father passed away was used to provide for me and put a roof over my head. I share this because I had a great deal of resentment toward all of them: my dead father, overwhelmed and overworked mother, and narcissist sexual predator stepfather. It was a toxic and dysfunctional situation.

It is hard for me now to believe this abuse happened for four years. I had had enough when he asked me if he could put it inside of me. Fiercely upset at this request, I realized I couldn't take this any longer. I told him, "If you don't tell my mom what is going on, I'm going to tell her." I knew he was sick with his sex addiction or whatever perverted thing this was. I guess I was always afraid it would start to become so much more as I got older. But I knew I wouldn't accept these requests any longer and it had to stop.

It took all of my courage to speak up, but I had to. I was so afraid. I didn't know if my mom would believe me or disown me and tell me I was lying. I didn't want to lose her and my family. I knew this wasn't anything a 14-year-old should be concerned or worried about all of the time, much less have to endure and negotiate with an adult parental figure.

I was surprised that he told my mom. I didn't know what he told her at the time because I wasn't home to hear it, but many years later, my mom said he told her that he had "accidentally" rubbed up against me only once or twice while I was doing the dishes. What the fuck? I was mortified that he lied, and I spit fire about it. He had lied about all of it! Even so, we went to the Department of Family Services the day he told my mom. I was so ashamed, but I felt completely out of control and not able to stop the abuse. I was so worried about being abandoned.

When we arrived, they wanted to have separate meetings with each of us. I had a difficult time sharing with the therapist what he did to me, which included inappropriate touching, because I was so embarrassed. My stepfather met with a separate counselor, as did my mom. None of us went to family therapy together and I don't know if that was even required. However, on that day when I got home from school, despite the lies, I knew my mom believed me, otherwise we wouldn't have ended up going to the family services office.

For a short time that summer, I thought my mom was going to finally leave him. By the end of the summer, I was devastated when she decided to stay. It is important to note that he never asked me to do anything with him again. I was grateful for that.

I say we had a "complicated relationship" because I lived at home after I graduated from high school and then through college, as I worked to put myself through getting my bachelor's degree.

What makes this relationship even more complicated is that he saved my life when I was 23 years old. In October 1991, I had an asthma attack at home, and I waited too long to go to the emergency room. He found me passed out on the front porch after I went outside to get more air. He arrived home from the gym in enough time to put air into my lungs, giving me mouth-to-mouth resuscitation/CPR until the ambulance arrived. When he called my mom at work that morning to tell her what had happened, she was fearful whether I would make it. Because of her nursing background and knowing how serious this was, she asked him what color I was when he found me, knowing my brain only had so much time without oxygen. He told her I was blue. My mom told me later this is how she knew I still had a fighting chance to survive. It was traumatic, but I made it through it. Honestly, I believe I had a near-death experience. I'll share more about this in the next chapter.

I thought my mom must have been in denial for years that this sexual abuse had ever happened. I hadn't realized that she was never told the truth. She stayed with him until my half-brother, 10 years younger than I, was 18 years old. At that point, she finally divorced my stepfather for so many good reasons, it was hard to imagine which one was the final nail in the coffin.

At the time, I truly thought it was the test of my life. I held on to this secret and held in my anger and resentment for a very long time. If it weren't for the support systems I had built around myself—my high school boyfriend, closest friends including "the Biddies," and extensive therapy, I would have never made it through some of my darkest days. Truthfully, I had considered taking my own life at different times from ages 12 to 20, but I could never bring myself to actually go through with it.

Why is this complicated? I wanted a dad. I wanted to be loved by my family. For a very long time the only person who knew about all of this was my high school boyfriend. It took everything in him to not beat the shit out of my stepfather. Then, my aunt and her sons eventually found out, too. They wanted to kick his ass.

All of this was my embarrassing dark secret. To put it in proper perspective, no one talked about sexual abuse back then the way they do today with the #MeToo movement. Maybe as a guest on "Oprah" or "The Jerry Springer Show," but not in normal, everyday life. Even my best friends, Dee and "the Biddies," didn't know until I was in my late teens and early twenties. It wasn't something I wanted to share with anyone. The abuse cast a shadow on my life, and for years I felt alone and helpless to do anything about it. I was in therapy for a long time trying to find a way to move past it.

Years later, when they divorced, I finally confronted my stepfather about the abuse. To my surprise, he actually apologized to me. I was emotionally raw, having gone through years of therapy, to finally finding a deep, true love with Grant. I'm not sure why it took me so long to realize that I was worthy of being loved in all of the ways I needed. However, even at that time, this layered onion wasn't yet fully peeled. I still hadn't finished my lesson about loving myself and not needing the approval-seeking/people-pleasing behavior and emotional codependency that was a part of my relationships. I was an emotional caregiver, safeguarding the emotions of others in spite of myself.

REFLECTION

I frequently over-committed, and then would feel bad if I couldn't follow through or if I couldn't show up to something I said I would do or go to. Some people I've known in the past might describe me as flaky. A part of me was back then. I brought this into my closest love relationships for years and it is still something I work on within myself, especially when I catch the triggered feelings of unworthiness or what I perceive as criticism or rejection showing up again.

I didn't know how to tell people what I needed because most of the time, *I* didn't know. And I didn't ask for the same reason. I'm not sure why it was hard for me to even know what I needed. Advocating for my own needs was a very foreign concept to me. This was another layer of the onion that needed to be peeled.

I didn't want to disappoint people, but what I didn't realize is that this behavior wasn't truly serving anyone, including me. At some point, a friend shared a brilliant strategy with me. All I needed to say was, "That doesn't work for me," no explanation needed. She told me to just say it and shut up. This strategy works because people tend to respect it. The decision is final and not in any way wishy-washy.

Growing up, if I didn't do what was expected of me or if I disappointed another person who was important to me, I was worried that I wouldn't be loved. I didn't think I had much of an option to say "No." As a child I was told what to do; like most kids, it wasn't a discussion. This is the way many of us grew up. Finding my voice instead of being resentful and acting in a passive-aggressive way while expecting people to read my mind, has been a real journey.

Relationships are where we learn how to communicate about our needs and feelings. I was so worried about being abandoned that I just held on to whatever someone gave me from a love relationship perspective. That is until I learned how to love myself more. Getting to this point in my life has been one of my most difficult lessons.

Self-Reflection

Manage your boundaries and grief around people, places, and things.

1. Take an inventory of your relationships—positive and negative, regardless of whether they are family, friends, coworkers, or acquaintances. Is there anyone you have a challenging or difficult time relating to, or with whom communication in general is a challenge?

2. From this list, which relationships do you want to work on and continue to engage in? Which relationships are you considering letting go of? What are your reasons for this?

3. Are there any places or locations you are limiting your time around or not visiting because they remind you too much of your loved one? Are you drawn to visiting any special places (including but not limited to gravesites, places you've scattered ashes, your loved one's favorite hangouts, etc.)?

4. What about things that were important to your loved one? How are you managing and caring for their treasured possessions, clothes, gifts they gave you, and/or letters or cards between the two of you?

5. Using your *Companion Journal* and the corresponding exercise section, once you have taken this inventory, you will see what is on your lists "Must Change, Break Up Needed, Purging or Storing of Possessions." How can you love yourself and take better emotional care of yourself and know you are enough? That you don't have to put up with being treated in a less than worthy way?

From these lists we will evaluate and come up with SMART (Specific, Measurable, Attainable, Realistic, Time-Based) goals to create an action plan to move forward in these areas. Yes, this is hard, and yes, you can do hard things.

CHAPTER PLAYLIST/GUIDED MEDITATIONS

- "Unstoppable," Sia
- "Rock Lobster," The B-52s
- "Tupelo Honey," Van Morrison
- "All I Wanna Do," Sheryl Crow
- "Smooth," Santana
- "Give Me One Reason," Tracy Chapman
- "Save Your Tears," The Weeknd
- For guided meditations, visit SheilaClemenson.com.

RESOURCES

- *A Return to Love*, Marianne Williamson
- "The Call to Courage," Dr. Brené Brown's TED Talk on vulnerability
- *Daring Greatly: How the Courage to Be Vulnerable Transforms the Way We Live, Love, Parent and Lead*, Dr. Brené Brown
- *You Are a Badass: How to Stop Doubting Your Greatness and Start Living an Awesome Life*, Jen Sincero

CHAPTER 5
Parting Clouds: Forgiveness and Hope

> "Forgive yourself for not knowing what you
> didn't know before you learned it."
>
> — *Maya Angelou*

TOO GOOD TO BE TRUE

Grant took me to Leysin, Switzerland, to celebrate my 25th birthday in June 1993. It was an over-the-top personal tour because Grant had once lived there in his vagabond hippie days. We were in this surreal place with a pristine, mountainous countryside, quaint "Swiss Miss" cottages, and the sound of cowbells in the distance. It was exactly how you might picture it in your mind if you haven't actually been there.

This visit was a part of my very first trip to Europe. I was awestruck by the beauty and the meals we shared. Most memorable was our experience at Le Leysin, a phenomenal fondue restaurant.

The most special moment of that visit was during the sunset when our host Barbara played the alpenhorn, a straight several-meter-long wooden natural horn with a cup-shaped mouthpiece, outside in the forest; a magical experience. This was our dreamy life together. With each new day I needed to pinch myself to see if it was real.

On one particular day we were in another beautiful European village. I found myself questioning in my own mind, *Do these places really exist?* because they were completely a fantasy to a girl who grew up in the Detroit area. From where I sit now, I recognize these dreamy real-life experiences were the serene calm before the storm on the horizon.

TOO MANY TWINKIES

After living together in France during fall 1994, we decided to visit Leysin again before we moved back to the U.S. to begin our new life there. On this cold December day, we went to the ski shop, Hefti Sports, where Grant had worked long ago. He wanted to spoil me, which was nothing new. Grant loved making any day special, but he especially liked planning surprises when we were on vacation. This time, he wanted to buy me an edgy one-piece Bogner ski suit, which to my surprise was rather expensive. I wondered, *Why is he buying me this when I don't even know how to ski?* Well, he was all about being prepared for the best experience. I was going to look smashing, baby, while crashing into that snowbank!

When Grant helped me try on the suit, the zipper got stuck, and he said, "Uh oh, honey, too many Twinkies." I laughed nervously, realizing that I had eaten far more than my share of indulgent French pastries and *pain au chocolat* during my stay. His funny comment suddenly made me uncomfortable. It was right in front of the salesperson, and I became embarrassed. For perspective, I'm petite, barely 4 foot 11 inches, although I'm happy to share that my driver's license reads "5 feet"! So, it's official in my mind! I hated to admit it, but I had gained a considerable amount of weight due to taking prednisone for my skin rashes. I'm not going to say I didn't care; it just was far from my immediate priority.

PARTING CLOUDS: FORGIVENESS AND HOPE

I didn't realize how his comments about my weight would grow over time and become downright nasty, especially during the last six months of his life. One day in Kauai years later, when I was helping Grant into his wheelchair from our bed and having a harder time than usual getting his feet situated properly in just the right place on the floor, Grant looked me in the eyes and said in an angry tone, "You're fat!" I wasn't sure what prompted this comment because I hadn't done anything that I knew of. In addition, I know my cortisol levels had skyrocketed due to the stress of caring for my terminally ill husband. I didn't think it was that unusual for my weight to go up under the circumstances. I looked at him and said, "I guess I've eaten way too many Twinkies! I don't know who you are right now! What the hell did you do with my husband?" *Seriously? What the fuck?* While comments like this were infrequent, I still wondered, *When did I become the punching bag for all of the things that frustrated Grant?*

Verbally beating me up in different ways in front of caregivers, family members, or friends became a recurring theme. It showed up more often as Grant progressed further in his illness. Grant's emotional defenses were down. All I could think was that a negative entity or demon decided to wreak havoc in his body. I tried to forgive and forget his angry outbursts. I tried to start each new day with a positive attitude, as if nothing had ever happened. Over time I became more resentful of his temper, and it became harder for me to overlook or justify his behavior.

I hate to admit it, but I took it out on him, too. There were times I would yell at him, "Who else is going to take care of you?" or "Why do you need to be such a pain in the ass? All I'm trying to do is help you." I will never forget one day, he decided to scream his head off while we were in a ridiculous argument. I can't even remember what it was all about. I seriously thought one of our neighbors was going to call Adult Protective Services. I called the home health nurse and told her she needed to send someone over to take care of him, because I was going to leave and check myself into the psychiatric hospital down the street. I was serious!

About an hour later she showed up. By then we had calmed down. We were drinking smoothies together in the kitchen. This interaction was not an unusual occurrence in our daily life together, although this time was arguably one of the worst.

> "The art of intimacy is literally the art of the angels, for it is the art of learning how to fly beyond the darkness of the world. When done poorly, intimacy can lead to great pain. When done well, it strikes the devil in the center of the forehead."
>
> — Marianne Williamson, *Illuminata: A Return to Prayer*

THE HUMAN EXPERIENCE

I needed to forgive Grant for being human, getting sick, and ruining our dreams. Intellectually, I knew his illness was completely out of his control and I didn't blame him. However, feelings and resentments are not rational. I'm sure I was subconsciously throwing blame and having an occasional pity party for myself and our situation.

At some point, I realized that I was never going to be able to meet Grant's expectations as a caregiver or, for that matter, his wife. In my opinion, he held a high bar of perfectionism and mind reading for both roles. I believed my responsibilities were way too much for me and I was in over my head.

On any given day I might say to Grant, "This is what you've got from me today—maybe 50 percent." Either I was having a hard time staying focused that day, or I was experiencing my own grief or emotional pain and was unable to completely stay on task and show up for him emotionally. Physically, I was always there for him. But I cannot honestly say that I didn't check out emotionally on a daily basis, for at least a little while. It was hard to be on 24/7 for more than four years. The closest thing I can compare this to is having a full-grown man with the impulses of a strong-willed toddler. And like dealing with a toddler, it was becoming harder to communicate and understand what Grant was trying to verbalize because of the progression of his ALS. This was our devastating reality. I truly believed I was never going to be good enough.

Grant would say, "I'm just trying to make you the best you can be." Well, *Fuck you!* is exactly what I was thinking. I'm sure this came across as I was moving his hand out of the way or adjusting his penis in his pants or helping him get off the toilet or wipe his face after he ate.

Honestly, I needed to forgive Grant for his pain and humanness. I needed to forgive myself for mine. Forgiving Grant was actually the easy part. How could I be angry at him for that long? He was completely helpless and looking to me to support his every need. And then he would say something funny and make me laugh. And of course, all was forgiven.

I knew Grant was comfortable expressing his internal pain with me. I was "his person"—the one he relied on for everything. I knew he loved me deeply, and perhaps he also knew that deep down I would never leave him. He tested me and tried to push me away from experiencing all of this pain. I'm sure it was hard for him to show me his wounded humanness. How could I not see this? And then simply let it go? I was working hard at being the best caregiver I could possibly be for him.

Forgiving myself was the hardest part. Going down memory lane and thinking about the things I had done or said to him in my lowest moments made me cringe. I had to work really hard with my therapist on all of this. After years of working with her I was finally able to forgive myself for being so fucking human in my caregiving experience with Grant. However, I still needed to muster up the patience to show up in my own limitations, shortcomings, and all of the things I hated about myself.

"The key to intimacy is the commitment to honesty and to the radical forgiveness necessary in order for honesty to be safe. Forgiveness and acceptance are the powers that heal us."

— Marianne Williamson, Illuminata: A Return to Prayer

THE FUCKING LAMPSHADE

One day, I came into our home on Kauai after hanging laundry on the line outside. Grant was watching the Discovery Channel from his recliner, and I asked him, "Honey, can I get you anything?"

In an irritated voice he screamed, "What's wrong with this room right now?"

I looked around intently, trying to figure it out, and said, "I don't know, Grant. What is wrong with this room?"

He yelled, "The fucking lampshade is crooked!"

I looked at Grant as if he had lost his mind, then walked over to the lampshade and straightened it. I said, "Are you happy now? The fucking lampshade is straight!" Yes, I knew this wasn't only about the lampshade.

Grant was losing control of everything in his world. I knew he would have given anything to get up, walk over and straighten the lampshade himself. Instead, he had to depend on everyone to do everything for him. Honestly, I know that it was awful for him. Meanwhile, I felt like I was losing my sensitivity and compassion because I couldn't focus on the basic things. I lost my temper on many occasions. I'm sure at times I made Grant feel like a burden because there were days I was resentful of his never-ending needs. I'm not proud to admit all of this. There is a lot of shame and guilt in not being able to meet the needs or expectations of someone you have promised to care for "in sickness and in health, 'til death do you part."

However, I resented Grant's need to control every part of my life and how my time was spent. This disease was taking its toll on Grant, me, and our marriage. Yet Grant would not see a couples therapist with me. He said it was my problem. Yet another reason for me to be resentful of him. With the progression of his disease, I knew we were not going to heal all of the emotional wounds inflicted upon one another in this lifetime.

I lived in resignation with each therapy session as I attempted to come to terms with this.

TOXIC POSITIVITY

After Grant died, there were times I felt dismissed, ignored, minimized, or invalidated by the optimistic comments of friends or acquaintances. These comments landed as raw and hurtful instead of helpful, as I knew they were intended. I wanted to tell them to "Fuck off" after they said any of the following:

- Everything happens for a reason
- Your life will return to normal
- You'll find another husband
- You'll meet someone and have a baby someday

…or the suggestion to read the book *Happiness Is a Choice*, like it was my fault for not choosing to be happy.

My personal grief experience was the greatest life lesson in how to not be one of those people. It helps me to remember these experiences as I watch out for saying anything that can deny grievers their authentic feelings and instead hold space, even in silence, to support how they cope with what they feel.

Grievers know better than anyone that people going through grief, loss, and trauma don't need to be told to stay positive. Yet we also know how subtle and nuanced comments and actions can be when someone minimizes your feelings or ignores your loss. Or how blatant it can be when others encourage you to have a more positive attitude. Minimizing the fact your life has completely blown up and will never be "normal," whatever the hell that normal is, ever again. After the first couple of months, people you see day-to-day will go about their normal lives and forget you don't have one of those anymore. But remember, they don't know what they don't know. People are not intentionally trying to be malicious or hurtful. They are ignorant if they haven't experienced the kind of loss you have gone through. They don't realize the best parts of your life ended the day your loved one died. Forgiving these people for what they don't know or for what they are unconscious about is the only way you will be able to move forward to feeling better in time.

HO'OPONOPONO

The Hawaiian practice of forgiveness and healing—*ho'oponopono*—would have helped me years ago but I didn't know anything about it when I was going through my caregiving experience with Grant. or feeling the intense guilt and sadness through my bereavement.

I'll try to explain it so you have an idea of this ancestral shamanic ritual and healing practice.

In 1976, Morrnah Simeona was the first healing priest (*kahuna*) of her lineage who brought *Ho'oponopono* to modern day practice. She was the daughter of a member of the court of Queen Lili'uokalani, the last sovereign of the Hawaiian Islands. Simeona brought this ancient spiritual cleansing ritual to modern practice with a Christian influence, including prayer, confession, and repenting. Modern practice includes the concept of "karma," including past trauma we may have brought from other lifetimes, represented in the beliefs of reincarnation. In Simeona's way, people wrote down their problems and moved through the *ho'oponopono* process step by step to peace and freedom through forgiveness.

PARTING CLOUDS: FORGIVENESS AND HOPE

The idea of creating karma, or "what you do to others you will experience on yourself," reinforces the idea you are the creator of your own life, and you are responsible for your thoughts, words, and deeds. The process of *ho'oponopono* moves into the cleansing of your thoughts and feelings. As we are burdened by our fears, thoughts, ideas, feelings, and reactions, they contribute to our emotional pain and strife, but also to our physical illness. If we can acknowledge who we have offended or what we have personally done from the beginning of our birth to the present, in asking for forgiveness we can let this process cleanse, purify, and release negative memories. This comes about by cutting ties; releasing blocks, energies, or vibrations; and giving them up to pure light, whether this be God, Goddess, Source, Great Spirit, or whatever larger force to which you pray and release this situation. For someone who is more intellectual, or not very spiritual or religious and doesn't accept this idea, *ho'oponopono* might be more challenging.

> "If we can accept that we are the sum total of all past thoughts, emotions, words, deeds and actions and that our present lives and choices are colored or shaded by this memory bank of the past, then we begin to see how a process of correcting or setting aright can change our lives, our families and our society."
>
> — *Morrnah Nalamaku Simeona*

This healing process has proven so effective that Simeona has been invited to teach her method at the United Nations, the World Health Organization, and healing institutions around the world. I'm intrigued by this Hawaiian practice. While I haven't used it myself in this more traditional sense, I have suggestions for incorporating *ho'oponopono* into your healing process in the exercises below.

GRANT GRIEF DREAM #3

We're eating in a sushi restaurant and sitting next to each other across from a couple we obviously knew, but whom I didn't recognize. We're having a lively conversation with laughter. Grant isn't looking at me, but we are close to one another. I'm able to witness him in his "Grantster" actions, doing what he loved doing, making people laugh and having a great time. It was like going back in time to when he wasn't ill, and we were younger and feeling invincible.

When I woke up, I felt blessed to have had this time with him, but I always wanted more. My dreams of Grant came few and far between; a year or more would go by without an experience of him in this mystical realm we call sleep. I believe he was given a type of permission slip to visit me during my unconscious moments. It made me wonder how many times he visited me when I didn't remember dreaming about him. I prayed to dream about him more often.

LET THAT SHIT GO

Have you seen the sign with Buddha under which it says, "Let that shit go"? It can be the hardest thing to do when we're grieving—to let it go.

What are we letting go of? I think it's better to ask: What are you holding on to that is no longer serving you? Resentment, anger, regrets, guilt, unrealistic expectations of ourselves and others? Are you still walking around in your armor, hiding behind your mask or stiff upper lip? Showing everyone how strong you are and that maybe you're not even human, stoically walking around while drowning in the depths of your own painful feelings?

We know we're holding on to all kinds of memories. Some are priceless and valuable; others we would rather forget. Should you really be over it already? Should we judge our pain and loss? Especially if we're sitting in the personal experience of our world that is forever changed from what it once was. Normal life as we know it has been tragically altered. How can we be expected to just let that life—the one we loved and cherished—go? I'm sure, like me, you have noticed that yes, it is actually gone. You are far from being in denial about that.

You don't need anyone to remind you, either. It might not be socially acceptable to fall apart and lose your shit. At least not in public. But maybe that has already happened, at least in your own mind. Some things that helped me most during this time were connecting with kindred spirits, finding the time to get lost in great self-help books, writing and journaling my feelings no matter how irrational I thought they were, and exploring healing modalities that offered some relief.

REIKI, UNIVERSAL LIFE ENERGY

I explored Reiki when I lived on Kauai because I was intrigued by energy medicine and the healing arts. I was searching for anything that could help me in my grief process, and there was no shortage of modalities on this blessed island of practitioners. After doing research, I decided to get my first degree in Reiki with Shalandra Abbey, a Reiki Master with the Usui System of Reiki Healing and teacher at the Reiki School of Hawai'i. I was intrigued by the healing powers of Reiki, working with the energies. I was ready to learn the variety of techniques. When someone says they do Reiki, they work with a special energy called reiki. They transmit this energy using specific techniques and symbols. These are given through attunements beginning with Level I, Level II, and Level III, the highest level of Reiki Master. A Reiki practitioner can channel reiki energy into people and living beings, including themselves, for healing and spiritual growth.

Once attuned to a level, it is said the practitioner is able to conduct energy from the universal energy field into the human energy field. The energy is then transmuted into a form that is useful on the cellular level. This energy recharges and realigns the body, bringing more balance and holistic harmony to the receiver's body, mind, and spirit. This happens independent of one's belief system or religion, or the emotional state of the conscious mind. The body's inner knowing connects with the positive intelligence of the Universe.

There is so much we don't know about that which we cannot see physically with our own eyes. I have practiced these techniques more seriously at different times in my life. At this particular time in my rebuilding journey, I didn't think I was seeing much relief from my inner emotional turmoil and eczema issues; however, I was self-medicating in other ways which didn't help me. I didn't get my second Reiki attunement until I became sober in 2005. I hadn't yet fully accepted my alcoholism, so this is when my life lessons became more challenging. I'll share more in the next chapter about my journey to sobriety. Currently, I have received my Reiki Level III Practitioner certification.

INTO THE DEEP: NEAR-DEATH EXPERIENCE

I had a near-death experience in 1991 when I was 23 years old. I got pneumonia and had an extremely difficult time breathing. Around 7 a.m. on a cool fall day in early October, I lay in bed breathing deeply, trying to get in as much air as I could. I was exhausted from laboring to breathe the entire night with little sleep. My back muscles hurt, and I had no energy. I decided to go downstairs to see if a strong cup of coffee would help. I'd had asthma attacks for most of my life; I was used to having a hard time breathing, although this may have been the worst such experience.

As I walked past the front door, I decided to go outside and sit on the porch. I was sure fresh air would help me. If I wasn't getting better after this, I planned to go to the emergency room. The hospital was a last resort because I had been out of college for about five months, and I wasn't sure I was still covered under my mom's health insurance. The last thing I needed was an emergency medical bill with my student loan and not having a well-paying professional job yet.

I stepped out on to the porch and sat down. As I did, my breathing became worse. I remember thinking, *Oh my God, this is how I'm going to die*, as I passed out into blackness.

My stepfather came home from the gym around the same time. Later, I found out he had done CPR/mouth-to-mouth resuscitation, putting enough oxygen into my lungs to keep me going until the ambulance arrived. He had called 911 and all of this saved my life.

I didn't remember anything until I was in the emergency room. I heard someone say, "She's paralyzed." This freaked me right out, but of course I couldn't move! I fell back into unconsciousness without registering anything more from the professional who was intubating me.

I believe I was in another world altogether. I was in a type of waiting area with people who knew me, but I didn't recognize anyone. It felt like some kind of waiting/onboarding room in another reality. I was given something to drink in this other world, almost like I was in a waiting room on a spaceship. Someone was trying to help me adjust to being in a place where I didn't need any beverages or food. When I took the glass, someone said, "This can be whatever you want it to be at any moment, just think about what you want it to be."

I believe that my guides pulled me out of my life on Earth because I had lost my way and wasn't connecting with my direction or purpose. The team on board this spaceship would say things to me that triggered a wide array of feelings. Once triggered, they asked if I got the lesson. I felt like I was going through a type of evaluation to prepare me for whatever was planned to happen next. I had no idea what it was.

And then I found myself back in my body in the emergency room. My mom was there. I asked for paper because I wanted to write so many things down. I wanted to remember as much as I could about what I was told. She gave me paper and a pen, but everything I reviewed later was illegible. I did remember one detail: "The only thing that really matters in this life is the people you love." This message came through loud and clear.

I was moved to the ICU for a day or two before getting transferred to a regular room, all while being monitored carefully. I had been intubated, put on medication for pneumonia, and given breathing treatments in addition to prednisone, the miracle drug that helps you feel better instantly. As I started to feel stronger, I was allowed to visit with family and friends.

I knew I gave everyone quite a scare, including myself. I needed to make sure this would never happen again because it was terrifying. I realized I was given a new opportunity to live my best life.

Over the next year, my life began to unfold in new, amazing ways. I got my ideal first job post-college, working in human resources for Mazda Research and Development. I was selected out of 600 people for the position! I loved my new job. I experienced a hard breakup with my boyfriend at the time, which became a blessing in disguise. I knew deep down inside he was never going to be the person I could grow with in a relationship or be my best self in this life. He broke up with me and started seeing someone new. I was heartbroken, yet as I started moving forward without him, Grant Christianson came into my life.

I was grateful at that time to be given the chance to make things right in this lifetime. I knew I was fortunate to be given another chance to do what I came here to do. I knew I needed to work on my imperfections, humanness, and the codependency that I so desperately needed in my love relationships to fill me and make me happy. I needed to forgive myself before I could extend it to anyone else. Eventually, the healing extended to my family, including my stepfather who saved my life.

REFLECTION

According to Marianne Williamson's book *Illuminata: A Return to Prayer*, all of our feelings—positive and negative—need to be processed and experienced before they can be transformed into acceptance. I was on a journey, emotionally moving through all of my negative, dark feelings in overwhelming levels of emotional pain. My caregiving journey with Grant and our relationship had been put through intense tests over time. While love won in the end, I also needed to forgive other people in my life who couldn't be there for us in the ways we needed them to be. I may have been disappointed, but I needed to let it go.

Managing my high expectations was a challenge. I needed to be gentler with myself, to check my own needs and feelings, and my unrealistic expectations of Grant, but also those of my other loved ones. If they weren't able to be there for us or for me, for whatever reason, that didn't mean they didn't love me. It's easier to judge others when you don't know the entire story about what they have going on in their lives or their own triggers. It takes empathy to step out of your own situation, into that of another to learn what is happening for them. At that time, I was short on empathy because mine had already been used up with Grant. I needed to find more of that.

I worked with my therapist for years on the anger and resentment that had been building up over a lifetime. This needed to be my focus if I was ever going to make it through this experience and my grief journey successfully. I've discovered many resources over time, which I'll include in the following Self-Reflection and Resources sections and in the *Over the Rainbow Companion Journal*.

In my opinion, forgiveness is the hardest work we will ever do. Forgiving others for the pain they have caused us can seem insurmountable. But to finally step into our own power and forgive the humanness or mistakes of others, and then to forgive our own faults or shortcomings, are the greatest gifts of emotional freedom we can give ourselves. We need to work on this consistently both within ourselves and in our close relationships. I knew that if I wanted to have healthy relationships moving forward, I needed to work on forgiving myself and the people I loved and wanted to have in my life.

Self-Reflection

Do your work on forgiving your own mistakes and humanness, and then try your best to do this for the important relationships with others in your life. Manage your expectations of yourself and the expectations you hold of your loved ones.

We each have our own grief story, and you might notice unfinished aspects of your personal losses over your lifetime and unexpressed losses in your relationships. You can do a deeper dive and notice where each loss has brought you emotionally to where you are now in the present.

What helped you get through the many losses of your life? There is a timeline and guide in the *Over the Rainbow Companion Journal* to help you.

LET THAT SHIT GO

What do you need to do to put one thing behind you today to "let that shit go"?

What are you willing to let go?

PARTING CLOUDS: FORGIVENESS AND HOPE

Go to the *Over the Rainbow Companion Journal* and let's work on this one thing you can do today.

Ho'oponopono

Use conscious language:

I let go of _____ (a commitment to yourself)

and I bring in _____
_____ (a positive affirmation).

The practice of *ho'oponopono* is the key to accepting our human imperfections and limitations in an effort to grow spiritually and to support the evolution of our soul's development. If you believe we come here to this life to learn valuable soul lessons, this can help you to make more sense of your human experience on this Earth and being in the world at this time.

This is a powerful practice that takes place in letting go of the story you tell yourself that isn't true. It transforms the energetic cord you are carrying around into the light. You can use this practice for anything that doesn't serve your highest good, whenever you need it, throughout your entire lifetime.

OVER THE RAINBOW

CHAPTER PLAYLIST/GUIDED MEDITATIONS

- "Apologize," One Republic
- "Hello," Adele
- For guided meditations, visit SheilaClemenson.com.

RESOURCES

- *Illuminata: A Return to Prayer*, Marianne Williamson
- *The Grief Recovery Handbook: The Action Program for Moving Beyond Death, Divorce and Other Losses, Including Health, Career and Faith*, John W. James and Russell Friedman, founders of The Grief Recovery Institute, griefrecoverymethod.com.
- Information and guidance on the practice of ho'oponopono:
  - self-i-dentity-through-hooponopono.com
  - self-i-dentity-through-hooponopono.com/morrnahs-questions-and-answers
  - self-i-dentity-through-hooponopono.com/free-videos
  - *The Book of Ho'oponopono: The Hawaiian Practice of Forgiveness and Healing*, Luc Bodin, M.D., Nathalie Bodin Lamboy, and Jean Graciet

CHAPTER 6

Riding the Wave: Rebirth and Transformation

"You cannot swim for new horizons until you have courage to lose sight of the shore."

— *William Faulkner*

"When we have the courage to walk into our story and own it, we get to write the ending. And when we don't own our stories of failure, setbacks and hurt, they own us."

— *Dr. Brené Brown*

WAILUA HOMESTEADS

About a year after Grant died, I purchased my new home in the Wailua Homesteads on the east side of the island. It was a five-bedroom, two-bath home with a *lanai*, also known as a balcony, from my master bedroom overlooking Queen's Throne and a dramatic view of Nounou Mountain. It was hard to believe that I could afford to buy a home on Kauai, but I was fortunate to inherit the money from Grant's life insurance, which exactly covered the 20 percent down payment. That was all I needed.

It helped that I had a ready-to-move-in roommate, Holly, to share expenses. In addition, with no shortage of visitors to the island, I could rent out the other rooms and make extra money. It ended up being a sweet arrangement, an Airbnb before that existed. I lucked out with a beautiful home, nice neighbors, and a gathering place for my *ohana*. Looking out my windows at the gorgeous view and lush tropical trees, smelling a hint of plumeria in the air from the tree in my yard, I didn't think I would ever leave my island. It was my home and I loved everything about it.

I loved and treasured my *ohana* more than anything. There was always someone to have morning coffee with and I never felt alone. Being close to nurturing friends, while having a few as roommates, supported my healing process. I had a happy home with a lot of wonderful friends and visitors coming and going all the time. I was blessed and grateful to be at this place in my "new" life.

HEALING PALMS OF KAUAI

Shortly after moving into my new home, I was accepted into the master's program in social work at the University of Hawai'i. I was fortunate the program was being held in Kauai for its two-year duration. This was the perfect opportunity for me to officially receive the qualifications for a subject matter I knew so well from my caregiving experience with Grant: medical social work. But unfortunately, shortly before I had planned to start, the university made the decision to move the program back to Oahu. I was disappointed, because I realized I didn't want to move to another island or travel as much as would be required. I wasn't ready to leave my *ohana*. My life seemed to be falling into place here better than I could have imagined.

Instead, I applied for a store manager position at Grande's Gems with my dear friend, whose family owned the most gorgeous jewelry stores on the island. I was fortunate to get the job, and this became my career for the next couple of years. It was a ridiculously fun job for someone who loved jewelry. I could hang out with the tourists and play with and sell amazing creations. Everyone was in a great mood because they were on vacation. For a while each day, I was surrounded by the beauty and *aloha* spirit of the Marriott resort, Coconut Marketplace, and Kilohana Plantation. This became the perfect position for me while I rebuilt my life, filled with *aloha*, support, and nurturing.

After a couple of years, I needed a change. I decided to move my sales position to part-time and start a nonprofit retreat experience that I called Healing Palms of Kauai, with the tagline "Because Caregivers Need Care, Too." At this time, I was attracting guests to my home who were in need of healing connection and a loving atmosphere with *ohana*. I had no shortage of passion and entrepreneurial spirit. I wanted to help people; I just wasn't sure how I was going to make any money with this endeavor, though money wasn't the reason I was doing this work. I wanted to help people who needed it, just like I did.

I wasn't too concerned for a while, because the bills were getting paid for the most part. Until they weren't, and I started to put more things on credit cards. This is another lesson I needed to learn. You can't start a business like this on a wing and a prayer. I realized it was important to make money. So, I transferred the nonprofit to an S Corporation and made it a grief retreat business that later rolled into grief wellness coaching for a few years.

It was a surprise to me when suddenly, the island became energetically still around me. My roommates, who were also dear friends, made plans to move out and on to the next stage of their lives. I reflected on the thought of leaving the island to build a new life for myself. I wasn't having any success finding a guy who wanted to build a future with me on the island, and this became more important to me. I was so frustrated that I couldn't find someone. Looking back now, I don't think I was in the right place within myself to find this person. But I couldn't see this at the time. I knew I was on an emotional roller coaster of dating different men who weren't emotionally available. You're already familiar with my party girl, drunken craziness from another chapter. There was more of that.

While this was all happening, my mom moved to Santa Fe, New Mexico, with her new husband. They were in the early stages of launching a Visiting Angels Home Care for Seniors franchise. As it turned out, they had a cottage separate from their home on the property that was perfect for a rental. After talking with her further, I discovered my mom needed help in marketing, public relations, human resources, and scheduling staff and caregivers. All of these duties comprised my expertise and skills. It seemed like a perfect way to integrate back onto the mainland. Unless you have experienced something like this—moving from a more remote place or another country—you can only imagine how difficult it is to leave the slower pace of island life, a different culture from the "mainland mentality." I call this the faster pace of life and the "keeping up with the Joneses" lifestyle.

From a professional perspective, I was ready for a new direction, but I wasn't sure exactly what that was. I knew and felt that Mother Kaua'i was gently nudging me to leave the island. If you talk with *Kama'aina* (Hawai'i residents), they will tell you this is a real phenomenon. When you have finished your purpose of being on the island, you know it's time to leave. I knew it was always going to be my refuge, a sacred place of healing and rejuvenation. I also knew I was supposed to bring others to this magical, healing island.

A part of me was sad that Kauai wasn't the best location for me to spread my wings and grow, for many different reasons. The island was small, expensive, and diverse opportunities were not as plentiful as on the mainland. In my experience, I needed more variety, which included all of the seasons. I needed the opportunity to spend more time with my family and mainland friends that were only a short drive or flight away. And finally, I'd had enough of dating, or whatever you want to call what I was doing on the island. I was determined to find my beloved.

RIDING THE WAVE: REBIRTH AND TRANSFORMATION

I couldn't believe I had an instant home and job in Santa Fe, New Mexico! After not much deliberation, because I felt stuck in my life on Kauai, I decided it was time to leave the island and begin a new life in Santa Fe. Everything fell into place effortlessly for me to move there. I sold my home in three days at a great price that got me out of debt. My *ohana* had a touching going away party for me. We promised to see each other as much as possible over the long distance. It was emotionally painful to leave my island. But I knew in my heart it was the right thing to do at that time in my life. I decided to bring Healing Palms of Kauai with me. My original plan was to visit Kauai a few times a year with my retreat business. Although this didn't go as planned, I was able to do a little of this while building an excellent couch surfing portfolio. As a previous homeowner with many guests, I was fortunate to have great *ohana* guest karma with many places to stay during my trips back to my "heart home."

Little Syd and I got on a plane to Santa Fe via Denver for our next chapter. When people ask me, "If you could do anything over again, what would you do?" Well, with hindsight being 20/20, I would have never sold my Kauai home! I should have hired a property management company to take care of it for me. It is my biggest regret. It would have been one of my best investments. However, to be realistic, I was in no emotional headspace to make that decision back then.

Overall, I needed to find my new life, wherever that was. I trusted that I would be led exactly where I needed to go in time. It was the best time for me to make this big move.

VISITING ANGELS

I became a Visiting Angel with my mom's business. Not many people can call themselves this! Actually, I had the title Director of Human Resources and Marketing, bringing my years of experience to the job in both areas. I looked forward to stretching myself in some new ways and it was a great opportunity to spend time with my mom, and hopefully build a stronger emotional connection in our relationship.

We had special times as a mother/daughter professional team in Santa Fe. My mom and I were able to have spontaneous lunches on Canyon Road, a charming street with art galleries, shops, and restaurants, and if we got lucky, shop on the Plaza in the downtown area between client calls. This was my first taste of working for a business with flexible hours, and I loved it. Of course, we were available 24/7 for the clients, so it was easy to justify taking time off during weekdays to enjoy ourselves when there were fewer tourists around. We did this when we weren't working our asses off all hours of the day and night to make sure we had enough caregivers to meet our clients' needs. Surprisingly, my mom was an ideal boss. She didn't micromanage me and we got along very well most of the time. We were a blessing in each other's life. It was the best time to grow closer in our relationship and to do the healing we needed to do together. I'm so grateful we had that cherished time together.

As a Visiting Angel, I did a bit of caregiving myself, as needed. The biggest personal stretch for me included caring for a middle-aged woman with ALS and training a couple of our caregivers to care for her appropriately. Sadly, my mom and I had terminally ill patients with Visiting Angels. We had an older gentleman with ALS, too. Going into the trenches again was a daunting experience, but I quickly was able to see how far I had come in my personal healing process. Caregiving was second nature to me, and it was easy for me to share compassion and empathy through my caregiving and grief journey. I didn't fall apart, run out of there like a basket case, or inappropriately break down in tears. I considered this a monumental accomplishment! I think it was helpful that I had been accepted into the Kauai Hospice volunteer training program a couple of months before I left the island, which gave me additional tools and insights about going into people's homes and supporting others in the needs of death and dying.

I was fully into living the life work I was supposed to be doing at this point in my own healing experience.

CHANCE ENCOUNTER #2

My mom and I had extra time one business day for a relaxing lunch. We decided to go to Canyon Road to a restaurant we loved called Celebrations. It was across the street from my favorite jewelry store and other cute shops, and we made an afternoon of it. It wasn't a busy day, so we were able to be seated right away. While we waited for our food, I noticed a gentleman enjoying lunch with an attractive woman at a table across the room from us. Holy crap! This guy resembled Grant, mostly with the mannerisms he used as he prepared to eat his meal and conversed with his female guest.

For a few moments I was back in time to dining with Grant before life with ALS, sharing wonderful meals and conversation. I couldn't take my eyes off this charismatic stranger. I couldn't believe the similarities he had with Grant! Then, I noticed how they smiled at each other. I felt like a voyeur, imposing upon their special moments together, but I couldn't stop myself. I was transported back to better times in our life together. I didn't say anything about it to my mom for the entire meal. I wanted to keep the experience to myself to savor it as if he was in my presence once again. This brought a fun sense of wonder to my day and a huge smile to my face. I had a little more bounce in my step for the rest of the day with this soulful experience.

A ROGUE WAVE

I was getting my hair done in a trendy Aveda shop in Santa Fe, comfortable with my new stylist Oscar. I got so many compliments on my hair at this time, and I should have, because it cost a small fortune. I went to the bathroom before getting started. After I closed the bathroom door, I froze while staring in disbelief at the back of the door. Holy shit! On the hanger in front of me was the exact same off-white flannel shirt with navy blue cowboys and horses on it that I had bought Grant as a Christmas present at least 10 years ago! It startled me. What were the odds of seeing the same shirt in a completely irrelevant place? It wasn't a thrift shop.

When something like this happened, it would throw me off for a day or two. It's hard to describe the feelings behind these experiences. It was like instantly having a part of Grant back with me. I would reminisce on our life together and how wonderful it was back then. And then it made me miss him even more.

Reminders like these could put me in a tailspin depression, especially because my love life was non-existent at the time. I'm not sure what happened to me in Santa Fe because I couldn't make a friend or find a date to save my soul. I was terribly lonely when I wasn't spending time with my mom or working with our clients and caregivers. My life wasn't what I wanted it to be. I'm not sure why it was so hard for me to meet new people in Santa Fe. I felt like I was trapped in a vortex where no one could see me. I felt invisible.

THE COACHES TRAINING INSTITUTE

In 2004, while I lived in Santa Fe, I searched for personal growth and found the Coaches Training Institute (CTI) was hosting a training program in Denver. I decided to treat myself to this experience for my 36th birthday. I drove to Denver on my own and was invited to stay with a friend's brother who I had hung out with a few times before as friends in Michigan and Chicago. He opened his home and eventually as it would turn out, his bed to me during my stay.

He was going through a divorce. This man made me laugh until my stomach hurt and I needed that. At this time, our connection was casual, harmless fun, which I needed to make up for the serious tone my life had

RIDING THE WAVE: REBIRTH AND TRANSFORMATION

taken in supporting my mom with her Visiting Angels business. We were caring for the dearest people and my work was intensely meaningful, yet I desperately needed intimate connection and a change of scenery. He and I would end up being in a relationship several months later, and this is what finalized my decision to move to Denver.

As my classmates and I practiced coaching each other, we began to feel more comfortable in our questioning techniques. I will never forget one fellow coach who asked me, "So Sheila, when are you going to be bigger than your story?" As if gut-punched, tears immediately welled up in my eyes, a rush of heat and dizziness came over me, and then I fumbled to regain my composure. I had no idea how to answer this triggering question. I had been living my "Our Secret Beach" story for more than five years at this point. It rushed over me that I had become my story. Suddenly, I was embarrassed and ashamed.

Another interesting detail is that I lost my voice and experienced severe laryngitis during this time period. I had no idea why and made an appointment to see a specialist. I was trying to find my voice figuratively and now literally at the same time.

It became painfully obvious this person had hit a deeply painful nerve. She noticed and apologized immediately. I mumbled, "No, it's OK. It's true." But this realization stung badly. All I could say is, "I'm just trying to figure out how to move forward."

I had to own what she said, because it was true.

A DENVER ASTROLOGER

At this time of looking for answers, I was always on the lookout for new experiences with psychics, mediums, tarot cards, Destiny Cards, and the Human Design System. Any insights were welcome. One of my Denver friends had a spiritual intuitive who was gifted in astrology. In particular, she offered something called astrocartography, known as relocation astrology, where an expert astrologer reading your birth chart can see geographical points that can be used to understand your connection to a particular place on a map. This shows what particular significance the geographical location might represent in your life or the personal experiences it may hold for you in your soul's development, especially with regard to purpose, career, money, love, and relationships. I was absolutely fascinated! When I asked her about Santa Fe and told her I felt like I was trapped in a vortex, she explained to me essentially that this is what my chart read. There was little energy or connection to building new relationships in this location. I could work on healing what I had experienced and my relationship with my mom, but there wasn't much else there for me.

When she looked at the Denver and Boulder areas, she told me, "You can create everything you want in your life there." This intrigued me because on my first drive into Denver for my training program, I felt like this was my new home. Everyone was inclusive, friendly, and outgoing. Drivers waved at you and let you into traffic with smiles on their faces—at least that was my experience back in 2004. When I asked about Hawai'i, in particular Kauai, she told me Kauai is my money place and will always bring me prosperity and financial abundance. I was completely validated about this, as I was still planning to do healing and wellness retreats with Healing Palms of Kauai.

The only surprising and disappointing thing she shared with me was direct and to the point. She told me, after the reading of my birth chart, that I should not physically give birth to any children because all signs pointed to this being a difficult and emotionally painful experience over the long term of my life. I was devastated to hear this! I didn't know if I wanted any kids, but to be told this knocked the air out of me for a moment. Of course, she told me, I could make any choice and decision I wanted, but she felt obligated to inform me or she wouldn't feel that she provided the best service. She said I could have stepchildren or adopt, but the configuration of my chart was a challenging one.

It took me a while to come to terms with this part of my reading. The rest of it I had figured out. I was going to relocate to Denver!

Relocating seemed like the best thing for me, as my work was closing out with my mom's business and I fell in love with my friend's brother, whom I will nickname Filth because it is fitting for how our relationship ended. He helped me move to Denver, but we decided I would get my own place to rent for a while. This was the best decision I could have made, not knowing what would happen in our relationship. I should have known I was a divorce rebound fling. Our relationship ended in a painful breakup after about six months, over the phone long distance from Sweden. He met someone there he ended up marrying a couple of years later. My consolation prizes, like a game show contestant, were my Christmas gifts from that year: a mountain bike, snowshoes, a coffee maker, and spa day package. He was generous, and I guessed I should have let him buy me the tanzanite diamond ring I fell in love with that cost a fortune in a Santa Fe gallery a few months before. This would have made me feel better about him cheating on me, with who knows how many women, including his ex-wife. She actually called to tell me about it after we broke up. Of course, I should have seen all the signs, but I was infatuated and hopeful that he might be the one.

THE SINGLE LIFE IN DENVER

I decided to swear off men and the dating life for a while, a resolution which ended up lasting a couple of weeks. I developed a couple of good friendships, oblivious to the fact they centered on going out, drinking, dancing, and meeting more unavailable men. But I had a lot of fun in my party girl life… at least that is what I told myself until I started coming to terms with the undeniable truth that I had a drinking problem.

During this time, I met with a friend who was a spiritual intuitive. She said if I didn't stop drinking that I was going to kill someone or myself. I knew I didn't have any discernment when I drank. I would get in a car and drive. I'm not proud of this; I'm just grateful I never got in a car accident, hurt or killed anyone, or got arrested with a DUI. I'm sure it was my guardian angels looking out for me. I knew God/Goddess/The Great Spirit knew I needed help. In spring of 2005, I decided I needed to take a break from drinking for a while.

MY SHITTY FIRST BOOK

I took owning my story to heart and decided to write my first book, the story of Grant and Sheila. I spent the year of 2005 working on what I now call my "shitty first book." I call it "shitty" because I was emotionally processing everything through my writing. Kind of like throwing up all over and then getting it edited. It was extremely cathartic for me, but if you would read it, I'm sure you would say, "Yeah, it's shitty!" Or maybe you wouldn't read it. It was *my* grief book and, in my opinion, not the best one to share with others. Still, I took a year off from my professional life and immersed myself in this undertaking. The experience was different from writing the book you're holding now, more than 17 years later. As a friend once told me, it's a different perspective when you are several rings out from the bullseye. I tell people now that my 400-page shitty first draft of a book was my grief book. I ugly cried all over it because that was what I needed.

I needed to relive my relationship with Grant, the romance and beauty of it, as well as the harsh reality that we lived for the second half of our time together. In full, we had only seven years together. I knew we were lucky to experience a beautiful love story in that short amount of time.

I visited my best friend Dee in Nebraska as I worked on my shitty first book, an awesome stopping point from Denver on my way to visit with my grandparents in Michigan. As they were in their mid-80s and I wasn't working a regular job, I wanted to get as much time with them as possible. Dee was not only my best friend from seventh grade, but she also became the editor of my first book. How did I get so lucky to have her on this journey with me?

While I stayed at Dee's home, I struggled to come up with a title for my book. One morning, I spent time in bed thinking about different titles. While getting ready to go upstairs for my morning coffee, I heard the song "In Your Eyes" by Peter Gabriel playing on the stereo upstairs.

I was jolted once again by Grant's ability to send me the perfect song in the moment, but this time especially when I needed one! All I could think was, *WOW, and some women don't even get a card on their anniversary. My dead husband can send me a song on the radio that is meaningful and brings me to tears.* The experience was a profound, compelling message from beyond time and space. As I listened to the words over and over again, I couldn't get enough of the lyrics and how they fit our entire ALS journey.

I was in awe and completely blown away! I shared this with Dee while I cried about how meaningful this song was for me. I absolutely had the name of the book: *In Your Eyes.*

In the end, it was as if I threw up all over 400 pages, yet it's edited and in a binder. I needed to write that book to process my own experience. Writing and reliving everything all over again was a grueling undertaking, yet this was a part of my healing journey and I know how valuable it is now. Today, Dee still asks me, "Are you ever going to do something with that book? Because I hope you do someday." Maybe I will, maybe I won't. I don't know and that's OK. I do know it prepared me to write this book for you, which I consider to be a deeper spiritual calling. I don't think I went through my experience at such a young age to not share it in a bigger way.

THE BOOTY CALL

The first time I met the handsome younger guy who lived in the upstairs apartment above mine in Denver, we had palpable electric chemistry with a single handshake. The second time I met him, he was doing his laundry in our shared laundry room. He had taken my clothes out of the dryer to add his, and I noticed my lace thongs on the top of the heap in the laundry basket. This is when our dating began, a bit here and there, with movies barely watched and hot make-out sessions. It was fun and nothing serious, more like a "friends with benefits" arrangement.

After about a year, he moved to another building, but we continued to see each other for sushi or a dinner out on occasion. As time passed, I began waiting and continuing to wait for his elusive phone calls. I hate to admit I sat in my own self-pity, wondering what was wrong with me and why he wasn't calling me. We had several dates over a longer time period, or I guess you might call it "hanging out." I was in my insecure pattern of questioning what was wrong with me, when suddenly, it was like someone slapped me in the face. I clearly realized and asked myself, "Why am I upset about this guy not calling me? And what the hell am I crying for?" I reflected upon my life and thought, *I was available for my husband through a terminal illness as his caregiver for almost five years and I was with him the final moments in which he died. And I'm worried about this guy calling me?! He doesn't fucking deserve me!* Really, what the fuck was I doing? Reality slapped me hard in the face and I needed it.

My worthiness was no longer a question or based on a man wanting and desiring me. It was something I had carried all along inside myself. Much later that evening, when he finally showed up without calling and knocked on my door, I clearly told him that I wasn't interested and that I wanted so much more than to be someone's booty call. I finally realized that I wanted and deserved to be more.

As I made the decision moving forward over the next year to be selective about the men I dated, I joked about choosing "the entire buffet" and having everything I wanted in one committed, loving relationship. I was no longer settling for cocktails, appetizers, or just drinks and dessert. And once I made this official affirmation and commitment to myself, I set the Universe in motion to bring in more available men. (At least I thought so, but apparently I still had some things to work out within myself.) I put together my "must haves and deal breakers" lists and read every dating book available. I had an entire small bookshelf about what I needed to do.

SOUTHERN CHARMS

I had given up drinking for five months when I met someone. He was a Southern gentleman who treated me like a million bucks. On our first date he took me to the Flagstaff House restaurant in Boulder, a place where most people go on a special occasion, like a milestone birthday or a 10-year wedding anniversary. This should have been my first clue, but I loved fine dining and was impressed. When he ordered a bottle of Cristal Champagne, he didn't know I wasn't drinking alcohol. I didn't tell him. I thought to myself, *I'm sure I'll be fine with a glass of champagne.*

This was my first mistake with my alcoholic thinking that I call "my monkey mind." In Buddhist principles, "monkey mind" means being unsettled, restless, and confused. It insists on being heard and it takes a lot of self-control to shut down. I didn't have the slightest bit of self-control when it came to drinking at this point. The only reason I was successful for five months was because I wasn't fully tested during that time. I wanted to be able to have a glass of champagne or wine for special occasions. This is what I bargained with myself. I was only going to have two glasses and that would be my new limit.

This worked for less than two weeks.

Over the next month, I found out he was involved in selling drugs. The kind of drug dealer who had friends with homes in Aspen. Professionally, he managed a restaurant and was involved in building construction management. He was on probation for illegally selling marijuana, released from jail after being incarcerated for five years. I'm not sure what he did, but I started thinking he was involved with drug cartels. I saw so many red flags and warning signs; however, I was being wined and dined, drinking and being spoiled. He would pick me up at my place, open and shut my door, and have bottled water for me ready to go work out together. He was the perfect gentleman and he adored me. This is how I got sucked in.

Within a month, he left a baggie of cocaine in my bedroom, and I flushed it down the toilet. I had no idea what it was worth. I told him not to leave any drugs in my home again. Another two weeks later, I was picked up by a limo with other friends of his I didn't know to go out on the town. I vaguely remember partying at Corridor 44 and doing cocaine with someone in the bathroom. I had never done cocaine before in my life. I was sliding down a slippery slope to a place I had no business hanging out in. And then, I stumbled into the worst night of my relationship with him at a dinner party at Mao restaurant in Cherry Creek.

I had consumed so many glasses of wine that I lost count. I'm not sure what he did to piss me off, but I slapped his face and left the restaurant, driving to no particular destination while completely inebriated. I landed at Wash Park Grille, flirted with an ex-boyfriend, and drove home alone, hitting a curb, large pothole, or both and doing over $3,000 worth of damage to my car. Meanwhile, the ex I flirted with—Filth—proceeded to take a cab to my home about an hour later. Thank God we didn't do anything. I told him to leave immediately because I had broken up with my boyfriend that night and I didn't know if he would come back. Nothing good was going to happen, especially if the two of them were both at my place.

I woke up completely hung over the next morning wondering what the fuck I was doing with my life. This was when I decided I had a serious drinking problem. I went to AA for the first time that day. I had to get help because something awful was going to happen if I didn't stop drinking for good.

INTO THE DEEP: SOBRIETY

My sobriety date is 10/28/2005.

It seems so long ago, but with a lifetime of healing awareness—officially sober for more than 17 years—I'm committed and dedicated to living a sober, happy, and full life. I tell people I still dance on tables; I just don't take my clothes off anymore.

Being the fun party girl is forever a part of my zest for life. I wanted to have fun and fun always included alcohol, even if I didn't always get drunk. I believe there are different kinds of alcoholics, and I was the party girl type. I had revolved my life around the party, and drinking became my fun event. I never drank by myself. It was about going out and having a good time, until I blacked out, fought with my date, my boyfriend, or a good friend, and then found myself with a hangover the next morning, throwing up and full of regret about something I couldn't fully remember I did from the night before.

Like most alcoholics, I had a personality shift when I drank. With alcoholism on both sides of my family, I apparently had the gene to go down this path. If someone told me I'd had enough to drink, I would order another shot to prove them wrong. This happened more prominently after Grant's death. Before he died, I would drink for fun, but rarely to sloppy excess unless I wasn't the one responsible to take care of him, which was rare. My drinking got worse after Grant died, and you would probably be right that I was numbing myself from intense grief and sadness. I didn't drink during the day when I was a professional, working my business or volunteering. I guess this is called a "functional alcoholic." When out with friends my drinking was definitely dysfunctional, and I thought I could get away with it.

I would tell myself I was just having a good time, because I deserved it after everything I had been through. I normalized my drinking because I didn't do it by myself, so I was fine. Well, throwing up in a wastebasket at work with a hangover the next morning is not fine, unless you mean FINE (fucked up, insecure, neurotic, and emotional). Stumbling around drunk and pissing off your date is not normal, either. Yet that's what I told myself for six years after Grant died until that day I quit. The heartfelt truth is that I wanted another life partner, but it wasn't going to be Grant. No one could be Grant. And I wasn't available emotionally for anyone until I started doing the sober work on myself.

Here is what I shared with a friend when he asked me how I've stayed sober all of these years—things I've built into my life that I don't take for granted:

1. I married someone who supports me in every way, and he isn't a party guy or heavy drinker.
2. I don't hang out in bars.
3. I had to say goodbye to friends who were excessive drinkers and weren't good for me.
4. I needed to build a new support system (I did not use AA beyond the first month or so, but I'm happy it's there if I ever need it).
5. I remember the last day I drank, and I drove drunk and could have—but didn't—kill anyone or get a DUI. This was my warning, and I listened and wrote about that day. I have what I wrote handy if I need to be reminded.
6. I know my "monkey mind" and the thought distortions it tells me when I think I can have alcohol and the illusions around "I'll be fine."

REFLECTION

The biggest life shift came when my fellow CTI coach asked me point blank—"So, Sheila, when are you going to be bigger than your story?" My story was my past, but it had become so much more than that. I became my story, reliving it over and over again. Especially in the experience of writing my "Our Secret Beach" story, the second-place runner up in a nonfiction short story contest in *Redbook* magazine in 2000. Of course, the person who won the contest had a child who tragically died. I cannot imagine anything worse than losing a child. The award was well deserved, too.

My follow-up book about my experience as a caregiver for Grant and our ALS journey, with the working title *In Your Eyes*, had consumed so much of my emotions and mental headspace in 2005. The book was the most intense part of my healing process, sifting through my deep emotions and grief. It was everything I needed. I needed this experience to heal my soul.

It took me years to finally realize what Dr. Brené Brown teaches in *Dare to Lead*: "When we have the courage to walk into our story, and own it, we get to write the ending. And when we don't own our stories of failure, setbacks and hurt, they own us."

If we look at a master of owning his story, it would be the Hawaiian cultural hero Duke Kahanamoku, known as The Duke, an Olympic swimming champion and surfer. This is his description of his best wave ever:

"Strangely, it was as though the wave had selected me, rather than I had chosen it. It seemed like a very personal and special wave—the kind I had seen in my mind's eye during a night of tangled dreaming. There was no backing out on this one; the two of us had something to settle between us…there was just this one ridge and myself—no more. Could I master it? I doubted it, but I was willing to die in an attempt to harness it…" (from *Duke Kahanamoku's World of Surfing*, Duke Kahanamoku and J. Brennan, 1968, 77-80)

We might consider that a spiritual calling is very much the same experience. It is as if the experience chooses us. Would we accept the opportunity and magnificence of living this experience in this lifetime? Do we have the courage to show up and be seen? I knew I had accomplished this in my experience of caring for Grant, walking the ALS journey with him and then healing my personal grief after his death. And I was preparing to do this again in my new professional adventure as a grief wellness coach and grief retreat business owner.

Self-Reflection

Rediscover who you are now and explore reinventing yourself. Knowing that you can write the ending of your grief story is empowering.

The *Over the Rainbow Companion Journal* has its own sections, with food for thought, questions, and thought-provoking exercises.

Give yourself permission to enjoy life again; you don't need to stay in your grief all day. You can let yourself enjoy the sweetness of life and choose to learn and love big, despite the emotional pain. It's not about what happens to you in your life, it's about processing the emotions, moving through it, responding with ability, owning it, and moving forward.

All of this can be done at your own pace that works best for you.

Explore SheilaClemenson.com and TransitionsCoachingServices.com.

RIDING THE WAVE: REBIRTH AND TRANSFORMATION

CHAPTER PLAYLIST/GUIDED MEDITATIONS

- "In Your Eyes," Peter Gabriel
- "Into the Mystic," Van Morrison
- "Come Away with Me," Norah Jones
- "Just Breathe (2 A.M.)," Anna Nalik
- For guided meditations, visit SheilaClemenson.com.

RESOURCES

- The *Over the Rainbow Companion Journal*
- Transitions Coaching Services—"Rebuilding your Life" Program
- SheilaClemenson.com
- TransitionsCoachingServices.com

CHAPTER 7
Like Rain and Sunshine: Embracing the Future

> "Vulnerability is the birthplace of love, belonging, joy, courage, empathy, and creativity. It is the source of hope, empathy, accountability, and authenticity. If we want greater clarity in our purpose or deeper and more meaningful spiritual lives, vulnerability is the path."
>
> — *Dr. Brené Brown*

> "Courage starts with showing up and letting ourselves be seen."
>
> — *Dr. Brené Brown*

THE GRIEF RECOVERY CERTIFICATION PROGRAM

In late summer of 2006, I was building my grief wellness coaching business. I was pursuing a certification to expand my coaching tools, exercises, and resources. In my coaching specialization, a grief certification made the most sense. Although I jokingly referred to myself as a "professional griever" with my family and friends, I knew I didn't have all the tools I needed to support my clients through their grief journey. I didn't want to be a therapist. Instead, I wanted to coach my clients to move forward through the rebuilding process, while holding space for their personal grieving. I knew people would come to me in different stages of their grief process, and I wanted to have the resources to support them.

I found a program that was the perfect combination of everything I thought most grievers needed: The Grief Recovery Program from the Grief Recovery Institute. The purpose of the program is to discover the ability within yourself to transform the quality of your life, so you can complete your emotional relationships with loved ones who have died or any other loss, including estrangement or divorce. By "completing relationships" you recognize with focused awareness that an incomplete emotional relationship exists. By accepting your part in the relationship being incomplete, you work toward this acknowledgment, no matter how small your part was in it.

Recovery components include making amends, making apologies, and sharing significant emotional statements, which might include offering forgiveness. This is done by 1) making loss history and relationship timelines/graphs; 2) making lists—of persons living or dead you feel you need to apologize to, whether for something you did or did not do; or of persons living or dead whom you think you need to forgive for something they did; and 3) making lists of persons to whom you would like to make a significant emotional statement or to whom you would like to write a letter.

The idea is that by partnering within a grief recovery group or working with a certified Grief Recovery Specialist, you can create the space for this emotional process, identify what you need for your own healing, and then verbally express your lists and letters, getting these words physically out of you with a witness to share your pain and experience. Your co-participant or specialist holds the space for your sharing in confidence, to help you emotionally complete your relationships. The goal is to help you feel better and find more joy in your memories of that person or relationship.

I took this program to heart as a coaching professional. The assignments provided me with a positive experience. I was able to let go of many things I was holding on to emotionally that were holding me back from stepping into my best self. As a result, I realized how much this program would help others.

I was committed to helping people grow, in their own connection with themselves and through their relationships, thus having a more evolved understanding and better connection within their own heart. When I began my grief wellness coaching business, my programs were about much more than grief. Moving forward includes life and career coaching as well. Helping people to rebuild their lives and move forward personally and professionally has been my focus since I began coaching in 2006, and it has been evolving ever since. I'm bringing a holistic approach forward in this book and your *Companion Journal*. It is the unique perspective, insights, and qualities I bring to my readers and clients that I hope support you on your journey. You'll find a wide variety of Self-Reflection exercises in support of your grief journey in the *Over the Rainbow Companion Journal*.

ANOTHER KAUAI VISIT, 2006

As it turned out, I was able to visit Kauai about once every year after I sold my house, but never reached my goal of quarterly or three times per year. I was fortunate to coordinate a trip with A.K., my Aloha Angel as I like to call her, back to Kauai in late summer 2006. She was traveling from her native home of Norway to complete her studies in death and dying, including the grief process. She wanted to do more research with hospice organizations, and I helped to open this door of opportunity for her with Kauai Hospice.

We stayed at a mutual friend's vacation rental and worked independently on our projects while enjoying time to collaborate. This was helpful for me because I was creating my grief wellness coaching programs and working on my website content with my Kauai-based web designer, Michelle of Emagine WebMarketing. Once again, A.K. and I spent heartfelt time together in our end-of-life, grief experiences, yet in a more studious way than we had experienced flying by the seat of our pants at the end of Grant's life seven years before.

I reflected upon the seven-year anniversary of Grant's passing. It has always been interesting to me that our life experiences and lessons tend to flow in a circular way as we go through various stages in our lives. Astrology, Yogic philosophy, numerology, and other spiritual studies share how we have different life cycles, such as the seven-year (Cycle of Consciousness), 11-year (Cycle of Intelligence), 12-year (Jupiter return), 18-year (Cycle of Life Energy), and 30-year (Saturn Return) life cycles, to name a few.

I could see that I was experiencing a seven-year cycle following Grant's death on September 4, 1999. I didn't want to admit it, but when I saw the Denver astrologer two years earlier, she'd told me it would be seven years from Grant's death before I would bring another love into my life. This seemed like a lifetime, and I didn't want to believe her. In fact, I did everything I could to prove her wrong. When I wasn't meeting and dating men, I was working hard on my new coaching business.

I experienced many levels of professional and personal development from 2005 to 2006, while fully committed to my sobriety. Working through the layers of the metaphorical onion, I had gone far below the surface of where I was years ago in my grief. I felt I was finally in a good place emotionally and spiritually, so much so that I felt comfortable leading and guiding others through their own process. My personal grief recovery seemed to be verified through the expressions of others. For instance, when I ran into my former real estate agent, she said, "You look like a younger version of yourself, like you could be Sheila's younger sister!" I took this as a testimony to my inner healing process. Apparently, I had taken years and weight off my face and body! Years of anticipatory grief and the stress of surviving Grant's ALS had done its damage.

While it felt incredible to be healthy and alive in myself again, I was grateful to bring my healing journey forward to support and help others in whatever way they would be open to. I was in the planning stages of my programs, drawing upon my past and current experiences, creating, and facilitating programs to help others. I know this is what I do well.

SECRET BEACH DAY, 2006

Monday, Labor Day of 2006, was the seven-year anniversary of Grant's death. A.K. and I decided to spend the day at Secret Beach to take a walk down memory lane, connecting with this sacred place we shared with Grant years ago. Almost every time I visited Kauai, I made a trip down to Secret Beach. This visit was no different. However, it did not always happen on the anniversary date of his death. I was grateful to be visiting on the exact anniversary with A.K.

After we navigated the terrain of the steep path down to the sand, we recognized how different the beach looked. There were many more lava rocks to the left side of the beach, so we walked up to this area, secured our things, and used this area to ground us in the wind.

A.K. and I meditated on the beach, with the ocean mist blowing through our hair, sharing positive intentions for the futures we were creating for ourselves. We were both creating new paths professionally and personally. Neither of us were dating anyone. Yet we were invested in bringing new love interests into our lives. Secret Beach was a spiritual connection we shared, and it was a blessing to have this time with her in one of my favorite places on Earth. I thought about Grant, and while I didn't necessarily think his spirit would be there, because I knew I could connect with him any time and any place, I liked to imagine him running on the beach playing Frisbee, hearing his laughter in the distance filling the air.

I sat quietly for several moments, taking in the beauty of the breaking waves with a view of the Kilauea lighthouse in the distance. I remembered the day he proposed to me at the other end of the beach, and then his last day, as we planted his feet in the sand while he took in his favorite place once again. This special beach held many fond and bittersweet memories of our life together. I'm sure most people have a specific place like this in their hearts. In fact, you might even be thinking of your special place right now or making plans to visit soon. Much healing is available when we can find a way to surrender to emotionally being in a place we're called to go back to and simply be.

I told A.K. that I've always felt close to this place, like it was a part of another dimension in time and space, where in some ways time stands still. I shared my intentions of bringing a new man into my life and that I was ready for him. I didn't picture him looking any particular way because I had lost my "type" a long time ago. My previous type—tall, handsome, and unavailable—wasn't working for me anyway. I wanted someone who was respectful, kind, with integrity, not an alcoholic party guy, and completely emotionally and physically available. Someone who had a great smile, strong sexual chemistry, and who did something meaningful for a living. I wasn't as concerned about whether he had kids or made a lot of money. I wanted a man of substance, who had been through some tough things and could hold the space for my life—past, present, and future. I decided to entrust my higher power, The Great Spirit of the Universe, to find him for me. I had grown to realize that he/she/they were far more brilliant than I would ever be, and I just needed to get out of my own way and show up. I let go in complete trust and confidence with a wish and hopeful prayer to God/Goddess/Great Spirit of the Universe.

We spent the remainder of our Kauai trip reconnecting with old friends and visiting with my friends Al and Marcy. Tragically, Marcy was in the hospital, unconscious with brain cancer. This was devastating, as she was an integral part of my *ohana*—the one who lived next door to me in Kapahi, the one who was at my door with flowers after Grant died, the one who invited me into a rich life of friendship and community. It was hard to experience what they were going through and to see how exhausted Al was in the midst of this tragedy. Our *ohana* came together in an amazing way for them, which was no surprise. I found that I missed all of my *ohana* deeply when I had to leave and return home to Denver. Whether I would move back to the island was always in the back of my mind. It was a choice I could still make if I wanted to. But at this time, I had my business to jump into back in Denver, and I was super excited about it.

THE HOUSEWARMING PARTY

Grant and I had become friends with a special couple the first time we visited Kauai together. We met the Murphys through mutual friends, and they became a lifeline for us on the island. They owned and managed the clothing and jewelry stores where I was fortunate to work for so many years while Grant was sick and then after he died. Sadly, they split up and divorced after I moved away. In 2006, Joel decided to move to Louisville, Colorado because he had always wanted to live near the mountains, and it was voted the best small town in the United States that year. Lucky for me, I was able to reconnect with him! We went out to lunch in Denver one day not too long after I returned from my Kauai trip. During our conversation, he asked if I was coming to his housewarming party in a couple of weeks. I told him I wouldn't miss it. He said, "Good, because I invited the divorced firefighter down the street." I smiled, intrigued he had done this. After everything Joel had been through, he was thinking about me. He knew I was having a hard time meeting the new man of my dreams.

I asked him, "What do you know about him?" and he replied, "Not a thing." I just smiled. All I could think was, *Well, I've never dated a firefighter. This could be a lot of fun.* I loved firefighters; didn't everyone?

Two weeks later, on Saturday, October 8, I arrived at Joel's to a house filled with neighbors and an unbelievable number of new friends he had made in a short time. There were so many interesting people to talk to. I was having a good time when all of sudden, this handsome guy in his firefighter uniform came out to the deck and asked if I wanted to see the fire truck. He had brought the truck to show the kids at the party and it was a hit with the parents, too. I thought, *Well, hello! Yes, absolutely, yes!* We visited for a while outside and then he went home to change his clothes and return to the party. We talked to each other for the rest of the night. In fact, unbeknownst to us, we were the only ones still at the party when Joel came downstairs and said, "Would you guys just exchange numbers already? I'm tired and I want to go to bed!"

I gave Shawn my number and hoped he would call me. On my drive back to Denver, I smiled to myself while I listened to the radio.

I was replaying the events of the day and evening in my mind and thinking about Shawn on my drive back, when I got a call on my cell. I picked it up and it was Shawn! He wanted to know if I would go out to brunch with him the next morning, and of course I mumbled something like, "Yes, I would love to!" I was so excited that whatever I said didn't register in my brain. He was picking me up in the morning for brunch! I'm sure I had the biggest grin. As I exited the ramp to the main road back to my place, I decided to turn up the radio again and the song "In Your Eyes" by Peter Gabriel was playing! I thought, *Of course, it is!* And then I said out loud, "I'm not sure what you're trying to tell me, Grant, but I'm going on this date tomorrow."

That first date was the beginning of our new romance and courtship.

GRANDPA'S PASSING

My grandpa died from lung cancer in mid-October 2006. I spent time that year traveling back to Michigan from Denver to help with my grandma's care. Our family needed to arrange for enough caregivers during the day to support her while my uncle, her primary caregiver who still lived at home, was working. She was fortunate to remain in her home where she lived her entire life.

One day, I sat with her and massaged her hands as she prayed her rosary in her favorite chair. She surprised me when she said, "I know I can make it through this because you did."

Tears welled up in my eyes and I said, "Grandma, I wasn't with Grant for long, almost seven years. It wasn't 60 years like you and grandpa."

She was adamant. "That doesn't matter. You loved him. That's all that matters."

I was blown away by her words. How could she compare a 60-year marriage to what I had with Grant?

The powerful thing that I came to realize is my story and my ability to move forward through the grief of losing my husband was inspiring not only to my grandma, but to others who wanted the same. These connections melted my heart in ways I can't convey with words. I knew what it felt like to be validated, seen, heard, and witnessed, and now by the woman who was like a second mom to me growing up! This is what I want you to know. When someone is grieving, you never know how powerful the gift of sharing your grief experience with another will be. I encourage you to share your experience with others when you feel inspired to do so. You never know what someone needs to hear from the wisdom of your life experience.

A NEW RELATIONSHIP AND NEW BUSINESS

My relationship with Shawn moved forward in a more realistic way. There weren't intense fireworks all the time, yet I loved my time with him and knew he was as into me as I was into him. It was refreshing to have this strong connection and chemistry with someone I genuinely liked so much. The hard part was that I didn't get enough time with him. Shawn was Division Chief with the Louisville Fire Department, which was a volunteer position because it was a completely volunteer department until 2009. In addition, he had a regular 40-hour-per-week day job and traveled for it on occasion. Oh, and the most important part, he was a divorced dad with shared custody, raising two daughters, 12 and 10 years old. Holy crap! What the hell had I gotten myself into? Believe it or not, I had never dated anyone with kids before. I know that's shocking because I had dated a lot of people!

How did we manage this? His daughters and I shared our time with Shawn. This was a consistent challenge that tested all of us.

My relationship with each of his girls looked different. Mine improved with his oldest, and then was a bit more challenging and distant with his youngest. We all had our issues and I needed to respect that I was the new woman coming into the family, and he and his ex-wife had divorced just a year before I met him. I made the decision early on that I was going to be respected rather than liked, although the people pleaser in me had a hard time with this. I experienced many emotional triggers that pushed all of my buttons. I'm sure both of them did, too.

If you genuinely want to know how much more you need to work on your "daddy issues," I strongly recommend getting into a serious relationship with a role model dad. I was triggered more often than not, but Shawn was able to run away to the fire station! Seriously, he just left the three of us to figure out how we would get along. He said, "I will never make the three of you happy all at one time," and he was resigned to that. In the meantime, we tried to make nice with each other when under the same roof. I genuinely cared so much for Shawn's girls and wanted better relationships with both of them.

Meanwhile, my grief wellness coaching business was ramping up. I worked with more individual clients and my grief retreat Hawaiian cruise around the Islands moved forward with registrations for fall 2007. Life continued to go so well that Shawn connected me with his good friend Karen, who needed a roommate, and wanted to live somewhere closer to Louisville. We moved in together, with our dogs, into a condo in Superior soon after.

Being closer to Shawn and his girls with a little less distance helped as we continued to build and nurture our relationships.

GRANT DREAM #4

In 2008, I was given an opportunity to join a new job in a coaching program as a career specialist. This was an idea from one of my CTI coaching colleagues, and I found myself grateful to be considered as a partner for this opportunity. I tried to make sense of the program information to see if it was the best thing for me and if I was going to be paid enough money to take the time away from my grief wellness coaching business. One evening when I was struggling with the decision of whether to join this group, I asked Grant to give me guidance because he had been a phenomenal businessman. I meditated and prayed to God/Great Spirit to help me find my way as well.

Within the next day or so, I had a dream of Grant. We were sitting on the floor cross-legged across from one another. I was looking at these gorgeous, large sparkling gems in a jewelry box lined with black velvet. I picked them up in admiration and said to Grant, "I can't see these clearly, give me your glasses." When I looked up at him, he said, "You don't need to look through my old smudgy glasses! Use your new ones," while handing me a pair of futuristic angular yellow glasses you might see on a character in *Star Trek!* I clearly got the message. I needed to use my own perspective, which I did and decided to pursue it. It quickly fizzled out and clearly wasn't meant to be.

It is so funny that I had this dream of Grant after trying to connect with him specifically for this purpose. This is one of the ways I know he still connects with me, through dreamtime. Most of the time, I don't bother to ask him to help me. I respect that he might have more pressing concerns, although I don't honestly know how he spends his time on the other side. Maybe I should ask him about that! I think that would be interesting to know.

Notice that I didn't title this story "Grant Grief Dream #4." I had finally moved to a new stage in my grief journey. Dreams with Grant didn't make me sad. They made me happy to connect with him again.

HEALING PALMS HAWAIIAN GRIEF RETREAT

My first grief retreat was a cruise around the Hawaiian Islands offered by Princess Cruise Lines. I had a small group to host and invited my dear friend who was a licensed therapist to partner with me on this first adventure. It was a great amount of work, but completely worth the experience! I'm still connected to quite a few of the participants and I'm good friends with one of them.

The cruise ship provided a nurturing environment while caring for everyone's day-to-day needs, and the excursions promoted an experience of the beautiful beaches and sights. Our grief programs and breakout sessions were supportive and nurturing ways to connect with ourselves and the other guests. Ultimately, we were successful in creating the experiences we set out to share with our guests. I took in everything about it, to see how I would do things the same or differently, including charging more money moving forward.

MYSTICAL CONNECTIONS

My new roommate Karen and I had a great connection and enjoyed each other's company while giving each other the space to live our lives. It was an ideal roommate situation. Little did we both know that Grant would make his presence known from time to time. We would laugh about these moments, and thankfully my roommate wasn't too freaked out.

One day I walked through the condo after we both got home from work. Karen said, "You just scared the shit out of me, I didn't know you were home." And then she proceeded to tell me that she was walking into the kitchen and out of the corner of her eye on the way to the garage she thought she saw

Grant sitting on our couch! *Holy shit! Is he showing up now, too?!* She said the image of him was in her peripheral vision and when she looked again, it was gone. Then she told me about the conversation she'd had with him and that she didn't want him showing up and scaring her. As far as I know, that was the only time it happened.

On another day, which would have been our wedding anniversary, Grant sent me another song. This time it was "Drops of Jupiter" by Train. I received it on my way home from work just before I arrived at the condo. I walked in the door completely flabbergasted in tears and shared it with Karen immediately! I couldn't believe that once again the lyrics of a song could be so specific and meaningful. I couldn't stop thinking about it.

I know it might seem crazy, but moments like these made me feel like we were still connected in some way beyond this physical world. Despite the fact that I had an amazing man in my life whom I adored, I still needed this reassurance from Grant that he was still around. I considered him my best friend on the other side.

BOULDER COMMUNITY HOSPITAL

The economy tanked in 2008 and created hardships for many, including myself. I was single, supporting myself as a new business owner and struggling. I knew I needed to get a regular job, but I stupidly resisted this with all my might. So much so, that I needed to ask a great friend for money to pay my rent and bills. I'm not proud of it, but I needed to decide between putting gas in my car and buying groceries, then deciding whether it would be dog food (of course!), coffee, or orange juice.

I was helping Shawn get to his shoulder surgery appointment one morning at Boulder Community Hospital and he said to me, "Maybe you should look to see if BCH has any HR jobs for you." It was a brilliant idea! After I dropped him off, I checked jobs online and there was a half-time

HR Assistant position at the reception desk. I thought half-time would be perfect; I could continue to build my business. I applied for the position and hoped for the best, concerned I was overqualified.

BCH Human Resources contacted me for two interviews. I aced them and was hired! Everything with this half-time position fell into place, including hours and health benefits. I was moving into what I needed to do for onboarding in my new job and seriously, a busy reception desk is more of a challenge than you would think if you haven't managed one before! I got to know more employees at the different locations (around 2,000 employees total at the time) and I knew I belonged at BCH from the first day I arrived. I had an awesome experience working there until more than seven years later (yes, that number is coming up again!), which is a career and community loss story that I'll share in Chapter 9. The strong community at BCH made all of the difference for me getting back into my previous HR career. I deeply needed this position to support me through my difficult financial times, too.

THE LAW OF ATTRACTION

Beginning in 2005, I began studying the book *Ask and It Is Given: Learning to Manifest Your Desires*, by Esther and Jerry Hicks, and featured in the movie *The Secret* about the Law of Attraction. I had read many books written by Dr. Wayne W. Dyer, the best-selling author of *The Power of Intention*. Dr. Dyer had a similar concept to the Hicks' and had endorsed Louise Hay and her publishing company, who supported the Hicks' book. I was intrigued by these voices of Spirit connected to Source Energy. These teachings describe your vibrational connection to your Source and your ability to understand and implement your own personal destiny.

The idea is that everything in the universe is of a particular vibration, and every particle vibrates to a particular frequency. The highest and fastest energy is called Source Energy. Manifesting what you want in your life is about connecting with higher vibrational energy to bring about your own well-being of highest good. Attracting abundance and prosperity through Divine guidance comes in the form of the right people, places, and circumstances for your highest good, which helps us to live our best life. According to Dyer's Foreword, "When you change the way you look at things, the things you look at change."

Esther and Jerry Hicks shared their work in their quarterly journal, *The Science of Deliberate Creation* and in their Art of Allowing Workshops. They considered their work a hands-on course in spiritual practicality. I was noticing a difference in my life with this practice, and of course living a sober life. I was sure these two things together helped me to find more success and trailblaze my new direction.

INTO THE DEEP: LOVE AND NEW FAMILY

About a year after my roommate Karen and I moved in together in fall 2008, our apartment lease came due for renewal. This prompted my conversation with Shawn about moving in together, two years after we started dating. Although Shawn and I were ready to take our relationship to the next level, the girls were in a different headspace. Shawn decided to convene a family meeting. I felt uncomfortable and vulnerable as I got ready for this family discussion, but I knew it was necessary. Shawn was former military, serving for six years in the Navy, and then had managed and trained firefighters and EMTs. I knew Shawn's "no bullshit" demeanor and authoritative fire chief presence was bound to come out. He was never one to dance around an issue and this was no different. He got straight to the point.

As we all gathered in the living room, Shawn set the atmosphere. He said, "Sheila and I would like to move in together. I want to use this as an opportunity to clear the air and share your feelings about it, about her, and about us as a family. I want all of you in my life, and no one is going anywhere.

Who wants to start?" And then he called us out one at a time, starting with his oldest daughter and asking her, "What do you not like about Sheila?" This is where each of us ended up in the hot seat. It was emotionally painful, and nothing was revealed that we didn't already know.

How did we work through all of this uncomfortable change? We either worked through it, got over it, or kept our distance for a while. We had fun times and challenging times together. Shawn's youngest hated me for a couple of years and this was hard for me to deal with emotionally. I had to let her go. I hoped she would come around and want to develop a relationship with me at some point. Overall, her sister and I got along well. Do you remember when you were a teenager? I do. And I know it could have been a lot worse.

Over time things would work out; at least this is what I prayed and hoped for. Getting involved with a man and his teenage daughters is not easy, but I would still absolutely do it all over again, especially knowing what I know now. Good things come to those who patiently wait and focus on trust-building in their relationships, and I love them both dearly.

REFLECTION

I had wanted a new love in my life for years. It was wonderful when I finally realized this dream in my relationship with Shawn, and then got to build a new life with him when we moved in together. We became an instant family when I moved in, with all of the difficulties that brought.

My personal boundaries were stretched, in addition to my triggers from not having the family I wanted while growing up. I could see the challenges Shawn's girls experienced with their parents' divorce, and as much as I had sympathy for them, I was going through my own emotional baggage. It was a challenging transition, and looking back on it now, I'm not sure how we made it through those times. I knew I loved Shawn, and I was committed to staying with him and working things out. He tells me now that one of the reasons he loves me is that I don't give up! I'm not one to walk away when the going gets hard. That's when I move into what needs to be done.

This doesn't mean I didn't make mistakes and have my own regrets with how I handled things. Shawn and I had at least a couple of intense screaming matches, although we tried to do it when the girls weren't around. He knew how to trigger me unlike anyone else and hit those buttons without knowing it most of the time. I wasn't used to being held accountable in the new ways I would be as Shawn's partner. I chose to be with a grown-up man who was capable of showing up on the worst day of people's lives as a firefighter and EMT. Of course I was going to do things differently with this guy! He was meticulous, responsible, and ready for anything. He was exactly what I needed, very much the epitome of the anchor (he!) that grounds the kite (me!). He is the realist and I'm the optimist. Another way of looking at it is he is the Taurus Bull and I'm the Gemini Twin—the good one or the bad one, whichever one decides to show up in the moment. Shawn's analytical side compared to my emotional nature tested every boundary that we both had, from communication styles to expectations and decision-making ability… or inability, in my case.

What a wonderful opportunity for us to grow together! (Please read the sarcasm in that.) Did I really need to grow more? Shit! And finally be responsible and emotionally available, too? Yes and yes! I asked for the man of my dreams, and I got him in every way, whether I knew I wanted everything that came with this relationship, or in this case needed it for my own personal growth and development, or not. Shawn calls himself my "little rain cloud of reality." He is this for me and so much more, yet we also go together like rain and sunshine. And we know what this often makes…wait for it…hell yes, I'm going to say it… rainbows.

Self-Reflection

Go to your *Over the Rainbow Companion Journal* to Chapter 7's corresponding pages.

Take your "Wheel of Life" temperature today. What are you rated lowest in today, versus what do you rate highest on the wheel? Do any of these correspond to your relationships with family, friends, or significant others? What about your support systems or community? Take an assessment of what isn't going well in your life in those areas. Any room for improvement? Go to the next exercise.

1. What would you like to work on first? Sometimes it is the area you have rated the lowest. Sometimes it is the area you are most likely to see changes in first. Let's work on developing SMART (Specific, Measurable, Attainable, Relevant, and Time-Based) goals to improve this area in your life.

2. Are you ready to stretch your boundaries and challenge yourself? What feels uncomfortable and outside of your comfort zones?

3. If you're ready to explore my programs, go to SheilaClemenson.com.

CHAPTER PLAYLIST/GUIDED MEDITATIONS

- "Drops of Jupiter," Train (Imagining someone in spirit returning after a journey from the afterlife)
- "Titanium," DJ David Guetta and Sia
- "Lovesong (The Cure cover)," Adele
- For guided meditations, visit SheilaClemenson.com.

RESOURCES

- *The Five Love Languages*, Gary Chapman
- *The Relationship Cure: A 5-Step Guide to Strengthening Your Marriage, Family and Friendships*, John M. Gottman, Ph.D., and Joan DeClaire
- *The Seven Principles for Making Marriage Work*, John M. Gottman, Ph.D., and Nan Silver
- *Ask and It Is Given: Learning to Manifest Your Desires*, Esther and Jerry Hicks (The Teachings of Abraham), abraham-hicks.com
- *Super Attractor: Methods for Manifesting a Life Beyond Your Wildest Dreams*, Gabrielle Bernstein

CHAPTER 8
Winds of Change

> "When you can't change the direction of the wind — adjust your sails."
>
> — H. Jackson Brown, Jr.

200 HOLES IN YOUR HEART

In 2000, when Grant's best friend Darv and I traveled to Switzerland for the final scattering of Grant's ashes, we met up to share the experience with dear German friends Christoph and Elke. Christoph owned a lighting design business and was one of the best storytellers, weaving history lessons into fun, creative stories. He had a whimsical way of looking at life and I loved this about him. His wife, Elke, was a talented nurse anesthetist, and the most accommodating host during our stays when Grant and I visited Heidelberg in 1994. They were two of our dearest European friends, also visiting us in Michigan and Hawai'i during Grant's illness.

We all had drinks in a charming Swiss pub the evening before Grant's memorial, and I was feeling the higher alcohol percentage of the beers along with the effects of the altitude. Christoph looked at me in a thoughtful, serious way, and in perfect English with a German accent I loved, he said, "Sheila, it is like you have a heart with 200 holes in it. Grant's love filled maybe 150 of those holes. You will meet another love someday who will fill maybe 170 of those holes. Some of them will be the same and others different. You will move forward someday and find someone new who makes you happy." This brought tears to my eyes. I knew I would bring another love into my life in a different but fulfilling way again. I carried those thoughts with me as a beacon of hope that someday I would find this new love.

WORKING TO LIVE VS. LIVING TO WORK

There is a particular time in our lives when we feel like we are trapped in our own reality TV version of the movie *Groundhog Day*, reliving the same day over and over again. You get up for work, make it through the day, come home exhausted, and do it again tomorrow. Then you live for the weekend, try to get some extra sleep, work on the house, do things socially to have a fun time, and then do it all again the next weekend. I'm not sure, but maybe they call this middle age?! This is exactly where I was when I turned 40 years old in 2008. You can add the extra stress of being in a difficult financial situation, considering filing for bankruptcy, and needing to tell your live-in partner about how you got yourself entirely upside down. Throw on top of this mountainous heap two hormonal teenage housemates who hated you at least some of the time, and you'll understand the life I was living back then.

How did I make it through this? I had an amazing partner with whom I could be honest and share my embarrassing financial situation. Shawn was understanding and even supported me for a while so I could get back on my feet financially, which was the greatest blessing. I kept my nose to the grindstone and worked my ass off for the next several years, knowing I needed to get myself into a better financial place. I needed to clean up the mess I was in and be accountable. Then, I needed to prove to Shawn that I could be responsible with money. He was the perfect person to teach me about this because he lived a responsible life within his means.

I was fortunate to get another chance at being financially responsible. I took the bus to work for a year and didn't eat lunch out. I kept my expenses under control and didn't use credit cards until I could be responsible with them. I worked hard to get myself into a better place by building back my career in human resources while working in my grief coaching business. I'm really proud of accomplishing all of this, but the hardest part about this time in 2009 was putting off visiting my sweet grandma for a couple of years because I couldn't afford it.

I planned to visit in September 2009 to celebrate her 90th birthday, when I had more money and time off from work. I talked with my grandma every week and I told her I looked forward to coming out to Michigan to spend time with her. Sadly, my grandma had a series of mini strokes in late July of that year. Afterward, she was being cared for in a nursing center. We thought she was recovering well and making progress, but her health took a turn for the worse quickly and we were surprised when she passed away within one day. I was happy she had our dear cousin holding her hand and praying with her. I wasn't going to see her again, and I couldn't believe it.

How could I have waited so long to get back to see her?! Of all people, didn't I have the big picture in mind about how fragile life is and you can never take it for granted?!

I was so angry at myself. I had lost the opportunity to see one of the most important people in my life one more time to tell her how much I loved her and how much she meant to me. How do you forgive yourself for that? I eventually came to terms with it, mostly because I knew it would have been hard for her at the end of my visit to say goodbye to me for what might be the last time. She wasn't going to say another goodbye. After she passed away, I had to accept this was how it would be.

I missed my grandma, who'd cared for me as a baby because my mom needed to work. She was my nurturer, the one who snuggled me. She washed my hair and my dirty feet from running around outside playing all day before bedtime. She was the one I was angry at for not being able to do my hair in the "Cindy Brady pigtail curls." She was the one who got me addicted to watching G*eneral Hospital*. She was the best grandma in the entire world because she loved me the way I needed to be loved. We had a beautiful funeral for her and celebrated her life with a family luncheon in her backyard. As I came into the house, setting the leftover food on the kitchen table, I looked out the window and noticed two butterflies swirling and fluttering around one another. In that moment I knew she and grandpa were doing just fine.

To this day, my grandma sends me money. I found five bucks in the middle of the hiking trail on Mother's Day one year after she died. Extra quarters have spit out of the change machine at the grocery store, too. This is telling because when I lived in Kauai, she used to send me a letter with a $20 bill each month. She enclosed a note that said, "No one should need to pay $5 for a gallon of milk, so here's your milk money." My grandparents lived a simple blue-collar life, not needing much except the love they had for one another and our family. My grandma was always giving people a little money to put in their pocket or some candy for the drive home. Little gifts like this seem so fitting when they arrive and tell me she's thinking of me.

THE REAL THING

By April 2011, Shawn and I had been dating for about five and a half years. I knew I wanted to marry him a long time before this. When we first started dating, neither of us were concerned about getting married right away. In fact, at one point, we both agreed that dating for five years before making that decision is the best way to know the true nature of someone before you commit the rest of your life to them. I didn't take the decision to marry Shawn lightly. I knew the gravity of those vows. At one point after Grant died, I would have told you that I was never getting married again. I never wanted to experience that level of emotional pain ever again. But I was tried, tested, and true! The Universe knew I could be counted on to be there for those I loved.

I woke up on a Sunday morning in a crappy mood and wandered downstairs to get my first cup of coffee. Shawn was reading the paper and I just started crying. I experienced severe PMS, to the point that Shawn marked his calendar each month as a warning and picked up extra fire shifts because my mood swings would get so severe. I'm not sure why I wasn't on medication sooner. I told Shawn I didn't know what we were doing together. I questioned whether he wanted to get married, and I wanted to know what we were doing in our living situation. Shawn interrupted me mid-sentence and said, "Hold that thought, I really need to go pee."

I sat down at the kitchen table with my head in my hands crying and wondered, *What the fuck! I'm crying my eyes out and you need to do what?!*

He came back rather quickly, then got down on one knee in front of me and opened a small jewelry box that had the most magnificent pear-shaped sapphire. Before I could say anything, he said, "Sheila, will you marry me?" and then something like, "I'm sorry I didn't have the chance to put it in a band. I was trying to figure out how I was going to ask you. But I thought now would be the best time because I want you to stop crying and I want to be with you for the rest of our lives." I'm sure he said something like that, but my brain short-circuited and all I wanted to do was say "Yes!" and jump up to hug and kiss him.

He had bought the sapphire gemstone I had shown him when I was working with Eric Olson at his jewelry store in Louisville. He had wanted to surprise me. I just wasn't patient enough, or was I? Well, it wasn't romantic, but it was us. I called my family to share the good news. Shawn had already made plans to go with his dad to the gun show for the afternoon and his dad was on his way over. I stayed home making a lot of phone calls to share my happy news and did laundry.

It wasn't what I would have expected, but this was real life, and the real thing, not some kind of fairy tale. It wasn't a pretty story, like getting engaged on Secret Beach. But it was our strong commitment to our life together. This was the only thing that mattered to me.

GRANT DREAM #5

I'm waking up and standing next to Grant, and we're talking and laughing about something. As I look up, we're in a long white hallway. There is an elevator at the end and Grant says, "Oh no, gotta go!" and runs fast down the hallway into the open elevator. As the door closes it catches the back of his yellow T-shirt, the one I remember him wearing at Secret Beach when we got engaged long ago. The T-shirt then releases into the elevator, and I see no sign of him any longer.

What were we visiting about? I don't know, but it is the last time I dreamt about him. Interesting that it was also after I got engaged to Shawn. It was like Grant knew I was Shawn's now.

ESTES PARK CELTIC WEDDING

Some years, everything seems to happen all at once. In 2012, Shawn started a new X-ray certification business and turned 50, his oldest daughter graduated from high school, and we were getting married in June. We had planned a Celtic-themed wedding in Estes Park on June 23, not far from our home, but a long weekend getaway to the beautiful Rocky Mountains. Family and friends were coming in from out of town, some making it a vacation. It was a Colorado mountain wedding and reception, with the details falling into place effortlessly. I found a gorgeous dress, Shawn and his attendants were renting kilts, we hired a local Celtic rock and roll band named Angus Mohr, and it was going to be a blast!

As our wedding day approached, I had the support of family and friends with all the details. A.K. came from Norway, Dee from Nebraska, and Shawn's girls were in our bridal party, too. The Biddies—Nae, Les, and Rin—came in from their respective states and my brother, Scott, was my man of honor to walk me down the aisle. My sister-in-law, Sarah, was our Mistress of Ceremonies. She even learned a touch of Gaelic to surprise us in her introduction. Sarah and our wedding wench, Lisa, our niece and Sarah's daughter, made our broom to hop over and ribbons for handfasting. There were many Celtic traditions and special touches. No wonder people had entire villages marry them in the past, because it took a small village to arrange for all of these details! It meant more than anything to us that so many family members and friends traveled from all over to be there for us.

The morning of our wedding, while I was getting my hair done, Shawn knocked on the door of the cabin and said, "I don't need to see you or anything, but I wanted you to know that a fire broke out about three miles as the crow flies from here. It seems to be going a different direction from the wedding venue, so I think we'll be fine." *Seriously, what the fuck?! Three miles as far as the crow can fly?* I knew that wasn't very far, but I also knew not to question a fire chief, so I went along with it because what was I going to do? At the same time, I was cursing every four-letter word in one sentence. My mom was concerned about me and asked if I wanted to take Valium. I said no because I didn't want to slur my wedding vows. I didn't know what it would do to me. I shouldn't have been that concerned, because I probably needed it.

We were getting pictures taken around 2 p.m. and then heading to the ceremony site at 4 p.m. for our 4:30 p.m. wedding. Oh, and it was 102 degrees that day in Estes Park. There was no air conditioning anywhere, because it is never 102 degrees in Estes Park. They rarely need it!

Due to the fires, the entrance to Rocky Mountain National Park where we had planned to take pictures was closed, but the other entrance was open, if we hurried. And yes, we made it!

Our photographer friends Cindy and Brian took our photos, and so did a group of Japanese tourists, with smoke plumes from another fire, this one in Fort Collins, in the background. Now, the Estes Park fire had caught and was moving quickly. We heard from a few of our guests that they were being evacuated, while trees were exploding in the background. During this tree-exploding phone call I completely lost my shit in the car and started yelling at Shawn, "Are we going to get married today or what? Are we going to be evacuated? Is it all canceled?" I should have taken that Valium.

Shawn remained calm and said, "As long as we have Lisa, my sister, and your brother, we can pull off into a field and get married!" This kept me quiet. Little did I know that Lisa and Scott were laughing their asses off in the back seat. The day was completely out of control.

While we navigated our way to the ceremony and reception venue, I started to think of our guests traveling from all over Colorado and whether they would be able to make it. Where were they staying? Would they be evacuated? Roadblocks were being placed throughout town and we were diverted. Elk ran in the streets of downtown Estes Park. A bear was seen in the parking lot near the wedding ceremony. It was complete mayhem! The irony was not lost on me that I was marrying a firefighter and many more would be at my wedding.

Immediately upon arriving at our venue I saw everything was under control. Decorations looked festive, the band had arrived and was setting up. I began to calm down and realized everything was moving forward as planned. I'm glad that I wasn't drinking alcohol anymore because I probably would have been drunk before the ceremony. I found a quiet place to hide for a while to collect myself, get freshened up, and to meditate. My nerves were frazzled. I needed to regroup and put on my happy wedding face. Fortunately, my family and friends were there for me in more ways than I even knew about at the time, taking care of our other guests who were evacuated and needed a place to shower and dress for the wedding.

Little did I know that my sister-in-law's husband, Jeff, was playing all of the songs he knew with the word "fire" in them on his guitar, to entertain our guests while they were being seated in the courtyard outside. As we waited in the procession line, I could hear one of my favorite songs playing in the distance, "Somewhere Over the Rainbow/What a Wonderful World," by Bruddah Iz. Our moms were seated, and then the procession of attendants began walking to our wedding canopy.

I knew this was my cue to walk down the aisle. My brother took my arm, our eyes met, and he told me I looked beautiful as we walked down to meet my groom. Our bagpiper, Matt, started to play "Highland Cathedral" while everyone stood up for my grand entrance.

From this moment, I completely forgot about every negative thing that had happened with the fires. Shawn was smiling in front of me; our loving family and friends were smiling and there to celebrate this special occasion with us! My eyes caught Shawn's as I approached him with a big smile on my face. I could see the loving look in his eyes when he whispered, "I love you" into my ear as he took my hand and stood by my side. We professed our love, respect, and commitment to one another 'til death do us part and then we kissed! OK, it was longer than that, but you don't need all of the details. Finally, we were husband and wife. Then he surprised me by picking me up and hopping over the broom, a Celtic tradition symbolizing a new beginning, sweeping away the past, and literally jumping into our new life together.

Shawn had made cupcakes that our family had decorated with flowers. We arranged these tiered, with my friend Cindy's clay-modeled figurines of Shawn as his firefighter self, wearing his gear and climbing up the ladder to me as the bride on top of the small cake with my hand down to greet him. It couldn't have been more perfect, although they were probably melting in the heat. Our guests, many of whom were firefighters, watched the helicopters putting out the fires in the distance during our wedding. And of course, they said, "Best wedding ever!" We celebrated into the evening, eating delicious food, and dancing to Angus Mohr until the night's sky glowed without fires, but instead with stars sparkling in the distance…waiting for someone's next wish.

DRINKING FROM A FIRE HOSE

My career in human resources grew quickly at Boulder Community Health. I made the decision to dissolve my grief coaching business and focus on my

HR work. I was promoted to two different positions within a few years, supporting a team of four HR advisors, and then promoted to an HR advisor role in 2015. This role was a combination of talent acquisition/recruiter and HR Business Partner for eight to 10 departments, a client base of 500 to 800 employees, with a blend of clinical and non-clinical positions. I had earned my PHR, Professional in Human Resources Certification during that first year, and jumped in headfirst with employee issues and workplace investigations, including Department of Labor and sexual harassment complaints. I got trained as a mediator by Collaborative Decision Resources in Boulder, which helped me to show up in the best way possible for my clients—employees, management/leadership, and job search candidates.

All things considered, I loved what I was doing, but I felt like I was drinking from a firehose in terms of my professional development and stretching way outside of my comfort zone. I loved my teams and was challenged by the day-to-day work, relationship dynamics, and recruiting for hard-to-fill positions. The volume and intensity of the work started to weigh heavily on me, though, over the next two years. I was stretched to the limit, with a new boss whom I didn't know very well yet.

I worked a minimum of 60 to 70 hours per week over that year, whether in the office or at home, struggling to get more free time for myself and others, including my husband. Shawn had retired from the fire department in 2015. He was hitting his stride with more than seven years in his Flatirons X-Ray Services business. And the girls were now successful young women in college.

I walked into our living room while Shawn was having tea in his favorite chair, and he asked me about something. All I heard was, "And then I bit a bowling ball in half." Well, that got my attention! I stared at him. After a long pause, he said, "You are not present when you are home, and you don't have time for me anymore."

I couldn't argue with that. It was absolutely true, and I felt like my professional life was out of control. I was trying to do two to three jobs in one position because two advisors had retired and there was no immediate refilling of their positions. I didn't feel like I had enough support from my boss, and I was drowning. Shawn and I had a good conversation about what I should ask for in support and resources. I was doing my best, but I was falling short in my marriage, relationships, and work life. We started planning a vacation to Kauai because we needed it.

INTO THE DEEP: WORKAHOLIC/ PEOPLE PLEASER/JOB BURNOUT

In May 2017, I began to think that I had a big "X" target on my back at work. There was toxic dysfunction happening in my department, and I was treading water. One day, I walked into the house after a long day at work and Shawn said to me, "What have you been doing all day? You look like you've been beaten with a baseball bat!" I responded, "I've been doing employee relations all day." Shawn replied, "Maybe you should stop doing that!" And I mumbled, "Well, I'm good at it. And they need me."

Just because you are good at something professionally doesn't mean it won't deplete your energy and run you into the ground. I was buried and I couldn't keep it up any longer. I kept hoping things would get better, with promises coming from the top that we were going to streamline our processes and hire more staff. I was told by my boss that I would be doing more employee engagement and career planning. I was so excited about this work! I was doing my best to hang on because I wanted to see the light at the end of the tunnel.

Shawn and I were leaving for our Kauai trip the next morning, on a Friday in May, and I had been finishing up my work at the office. I didn't get home until 9 p.m. that night, and I still had to pack. Needless to say, my husband was livid. He was frustrated about my dysfunctional patterns and never being on time, and not being able to count on me for anything. I could see I was on his last nerve. All he said to me before he went to bed was that I had better be packed and ready to go when he walked out the door, or he would be leaving without me.

The next morning, I was exhausted, but packed and ready to head out. On our ride to the airport, Shawn didn't talk with me much and I could sense the cold shoulder. I felt defeated in my career and my relationship with him, going on what should have been a wonderful vacation to Kauai—my heart home. But I was miserable. On the plane, I thought about everything that I couldn't get done before I left and just wondered what I was going to get in trouble for not doing when I got back to work. I tried to watch a movie and sleep, but instead my mind raced with thoughts about work on a continuous loop. When Shawn and I arrived in Lihue, we got our car rental and made our way to the resort in Kapaa. I think we had dinner that night, looked at the ocean, and in exhaustion went to bed.

The next morning began on a much brighter note, with the sunshine and gorgeous tropical breeze. We enjoyed a breakfast buffet with ripe island papaya and mango, spicy Portuguese sausage, and omelets. I was beginning to feel human again and Shawn seemed to be in a better mood after he finally found hot water for the English tea bags he had brought from home. After breakfast, we decided to take a walk along the beach. I was relieved to be back on Kauai and needed the downtime badly.

As we sat under a shady tree overlooking the ocean, Shawn gave me a small box that said *Na Hoku*. I was surprised because it wasn't an anniversary and not my birthday yet. I opened it to see a gorgeous gold wave necklace with Australian opal inlay and a diamond teardrop. Tears ran down my cheeks. I was speechless. After everything we had been through over the past year, he was giving me this heartfelt gift? Then he said, "I know you've been working hard to do what you need to do professionally and I'm proud of you."

There was a long silence. I kissed him and he helped me put on the necklace. It sparkled in the sunlight and warmed my heart. That was when the conversation took on a more serious tone. Shawn told me he was concerned that I wasn't taking care of myself. That I had become a workaholic. He told me I needed to get another job and he gave me three months. He told me he wasn't giving me an ultimatum or divorcing me if I didn't get another job, he just simply said, "I want my wife back. I don't want just a roommate who isn't there anymore." Wow, if you are ever going to be called out for something in a big way, he wrote the book on the delivery. He had my attention.

I understood I needed to change how I managed my work/life balance moving forward. This was not going to be easy for me. I didn't know what I was going to do, but I promised him I would work on it.

REFLECTION

When I came back from vacation I was relaxed. This lasted about two days. The next two months were grueling. I had moved into a talent acquisition recruiter role for clinical operations at BCH. I was recruiting for 140 clinical positions—mostly nursing jobs during the nursing shortage. I transferred my job as an HR advisor to a newly hired HR Business Partner (HRBP) because my HR advisor job was being split into two positions in a new structure. I felt validated that I had been doing at least two jobs after all! However, my management team and the employees I supported were attached to me and still wanted to reach out to me for questions and answers about everything they were supposed to bring to the new person.

As a result, I was being pulled in too many directions for the number of working hours in a day. I needed to transfer paperwork to the new HRBP, and it was getting lost in an inefficient process. Suddenly, I was drowning again. The department had a toxic and dysfunctional leadership style, and I wasn't being treated the way I deserved to be treated. The final straw occurred in a meeting with all of my colleagues. I went home frustrated that day, realizing that I needed to look for a new job.

I thought about my new job search over the weekend. I was intimidated about getting back out there. Nine years was a long time. Even though I hired people for a living and knew what to do, it was still hard to come to terms with leaving. I had a pit in my stomach all day on Sunday as I dreaded going back to the office in the morning, and I had a sleepless night. When I woke up, Shawn came into our bedroom and I said to him, "Honey, I can't do this job anymore."

He lit up and said, "I'll go make you a cup of coffee and let's write your resignation letter." When we started on it, he encouraged me to put the difficult things in, too. He told me we would be OK financially for a few months and even though he was on my health insurance, we would figure it out.

I was relieved and then I felt like I was jumping off a cliff. I felt so sad to leave my BCH community. I didn't want to leave my coworkers and colleagues, but I was completely burned out and I needed to heal myself.

Self-Reflection

Embrace a new sense of hope, meaning, and purpose.

I worked with an amazing therapist and career coach who helped me piece my life back together while I was going through this career crisis. I was referred to resources that I've read, listed below. In addition, I decided I was going to bring my HR profession forward into career coaching and registered for a Global Career Development Certification class. I needed a lot of down time to process the emotions of everything I had been through, and this took a few months.

If you are navigating a similar situation, I can lead you through this in my programs listed on TransitionsCoachingServices.com.

CHAPTER PLAYLIST/GUIDED MEDITATIONS

- ❀ "Marry Me," Train
- ❀ "Brown-Eyed Girl," Van Morrison
- ❀ "Only Girl (In The World)," Rihanna

- ❀ "Highland Cathedral," traditional Celtic bagpipes
- ❀ "Somewhere Over the Rainbow/What a Wonderful World," Israel "Bruddah Iz" Kamakawiwo'ole
- ❀ "The Best Is Yet to Come," Michael Bublé
- ❀ For guided meditations, visit SheilaClemenson.com.

RESOURCES

- ❀ *Finding Your Own North Star: Claiming the Life You Were Meant to Live*, Martha Beck
- ❀ *Steering by Starlight: The Science and Magic of Finding Your Destiny*, Martha Beck
- ❀ *What Color is Your Parachute? A Practical Manual for Job-Hunters and Career-Changers*, Richard N. Bolles
- ❀ *Living on Purpose: Straight Answers to Life's Tough Questions*, Dan Millman
- ❀ *You Are a Badass: How to Stop Doubting Your Greatness and Start Living an Awesome Life*, Jen Sincero
- ❀ *The Art of Work: A Proven Path to Discovering What You Were Meant to Do*, Jeff Goins
- ❀ TransitionsCoachingServices.com, my transitions/career coaching business

CHAPTER 9

The Erupting Volcano: Unbelievable Losses

> "What is work-life imbalance? It's: I feel safe at home, I don't feel safe at work. That's the imbalance. And no amount of yoga or vacation time is going to fix that."
>
> — *Simon Sinek*

> "The key is not to prioritize what's on your schedule but to schedule your priorities."
>
> — *Stephen Covey*

LIFE WITHOUT BCH

When you are googling quizzes about job burnout and reading articles to see if you have all the signs, note to self: you are completely there already. The best analogy for me is a pressure cooker that starts at a low simmer and goes to boiling. You know it's getting hot; you just don't know how hot it's going to get until you are already there.

After I resigned from BCH, running out of there with my hair on fire, I didn't know if it was possible to ever have a position with work/life balance. I didn't know if I was capable of work/life balance. Sometimes *they* say—again, whoever *they* are—if you are an alcoholic, you will simply replace your addiction with something else, whether that is smoking, exercise, or in my case, work. I justified it because people needed me. Or all of the other reasons I gave my husband for why I couldn't tear myself away from doing something that was slowly killing me inside. I had to come to terms with whatever this was in me that needed to be needed, at my own expense. I needed to discover my own precious self-care and boundaries.

When I walked out that door, I had lost my professional identity and work community in one shot, and I wasn't sure what I was going to do. Because of the toxic leader in my department, I needed to keep quiet and not put myself out there to say goodbye; I was taking the high road and not trash talking anyone (who probably deserved it). I felt supported by upper leadership and everyone else in my department for leaving, and I knew I needed to take a stand. So, I did.

I had the opportunity to go back to open arms, but I had to do a deeper dive within myself and admit that the nature of working in a nonprofit healthcare organization and an HR recruiting position was slowly killing me with the stress of intense needs that couldn't be met. I couldn't separate myself from that because I was such an empath, having the ability to connect with the emotions of others, but I didn't have my personal boundaries in place yet. I didn't know how at that time. I had a lot of self-care to do, and this was my focus for a few months.

I had amazing support from a counseling therapist named Sharla and her husband, Dan, a former CTI colleague who was a career counselor. They helped me to put my pieces back together and connect the dots for my future direction. I took more assessments, did a deeper dive into the job seekers' classic *What Color is My Parachute?* by Richard Bolles, and then discovered that career coaching was my new direction. If I couldn't do the work I wanted to with an employer, I was going to create my own coaching business. This was the birth of Transitions Coaching Services, LLC, in January 2018.

THE ERUPTING VOLCANO: UNBELIEVABLE LOSSES

I started my new business while I took the career development certification program with my mentor, Linda. It is the best thing I could have ever done for my career and professional development. Then, I read the book by Shonda Rhimes, *Year of Yes: How to Dance It Out, Stand in the Sun and Be Your Own Person,"* which changed my life. I decided I was going to say "Yes" to every opportunity that came in to support my new business and career, whether I could see how it would benefit me or not. I did things that were uncomfortable, like giving a LinkedIn presentation for 100 women at Dress for Success, joining a leads group with the Superior Chamber of Commerce. and stretching myself into different opportunities through my networks of amazing women from Boulder to Denver, and beyond. I wouldn't have been able to take this opportunity without the financial and emotional support of my husband, Shawn. He gets credit, because he opened this opportunity for me to make my new life a reality. I've been blessed beyond words.

Little did I know what was coming in 2020 and how I couldn't have picked a better career or started my career coaching business at a better time for the changes we would all experience in our lives, the way we do work, and our careers.

THE LIFE- AND WORK-CHANGING COVID-19 PANDEMIC

On March 7, 2020, I attended Oprah's "2020 Vision: Your Life In Focus" at the Pepsi Center in Denver with a dear friend of mine, Karla, who was visiting from Kauai. We had planned this event since the previous November. The venue was jam-packed. It was the first time I was happy to be sitting in the nosebleed seats to the side of the stage, where there weren't as many people. It seemed surreal to be concerned about large groups of people getting together, but I had seen the movie *Contagion*, and this seemed to be the scary direction we were headed. I felt so fortunate that I was blessed by not being impacted by the virus at this event, as far as I'm aware. We were ignorant of what was coming; in fact, it was already here, but not as widespread as it would become. Oprah's visioning program ended up being one of the final events before all arena events were canceled. COVID-19 stay-at-home orders began in Colorado on March 26, 2020.

Our entire world went through this pandemic together in different stages, with the first outbreak in China to the first American case being reported on January 20, 2020. The first known deaths occurred in February. By mid-April, disaster declarations were made in all states and territories as cases increased. It was a terrifying time without a known treatment or vaccine and with a high mortality rate. Every country and state had its own protocols.

Our common experience has changed our lives and perspectives. We will never see the world the same way. There was so much tragedy, loss, and death. Although the world is getting back to a "new normal," many lives will never be remotely close to normal ever again. How are we holding the space for all of the grief and loss? People not able to hold their loved ones, not able to say a proper "goodbye"? So many fears, and very little knowledge and resources to figure it out.

Where do we go from dreaming about quarantines and wearing masks, or freaking out when you watch people on TV getting into an elevator together on a show like "Seinfeld"? Well, life comes back. I can see we're gradually returning to our groove. I feel much more relieved and grateful about our COVID-19 public health situation.

I want to know how people are healing from these tragedies. I want to know what they've done to cope and move forward. This was the main event for two years and we all had front row seats. There were layers upon layers of confusion and chaos without strong leadership. We were all flying by the seat of our pants while trying to do our best with the knowledge and resources we had at the time. We need to forgive ourselves for what we didn't know and any stupid mistakes we made as a result.

THE ERUPTING VOLCANO: UNBELIEVABLE LOSSES

THE MARSHALL FIRE: DECEMBER 30, 2021

As I write this book, my communities of Louisville, Superior, and Boulder are devastated by the trauma and horrific aftermath of the fires that surrounded all of us. We received the emergency alert on our cell phones and 40,000 people were evacuated in about two hours on Thursday afternoon, December 30. Unfortunately, not everyone got the alert and firefighters and police officers went door to door to evacuate people too close to the fires. This included my husband's ex-wife, and her home where my eldest stepdaughter had just relocated with all of her belongings from New York City.

While this was happening in Colorado, I was visiting my mom in Santa Fe with my eldest stepdaughter for a fun getaway. My husband was home with my other stepdaughter, who was also visiting from New York, and our dogs and bird. They all evacuated with everyone else in town.

No matter where you were, if you were a resident of these communities, the fires shook you to your core. You didn't know if you would return to your home when you left. The smoke and fires came in faster than one would ever imagine, and many couldn't get back to their pets, especially in the Sagamore neighborhood, where more than 370 homes burned in a matter of minutes with flames driven by 110-mph winds. Seeing what is left is shocking, with entire neighborhoods gone, foundations burned down to rubble, and scorched trees and ground. The last I heard, a total of 1,088 homes were destroyed.

My husband Shawn is a retired firefighter/EMT, and former Division Chief and board member of the Louisville Fire Department. He was put on call that day. Fortunately, crews and trucks came from communities as far as Pueblo and Weld counties, hours away. Firefighters who were involved commented that they came in and got their asses handed to them. A structure fire will normally have about 22 to 24 firefighters at a given time depending on the size. In this case, they had three to four people arriving on scene with seven to 10 homes on fire. The wind and fires didn't die down until after 5 p.m. The conditions raged for half a day, with flames running like a freight train around our towns. It is a miracle no firefighter was killed on the job. Tragically, two people lost their lives, as well as an estimated 1,000 beloved pets. It could have been so many more and the fact it wasn't, I would call a miracle.

We lost about 20 percent of our communities, but they saved 80 percent of our homes. Every person in our community has a story and was impacted by this tragedy. The Marshall Fire is the most destructive wildfire in Colorado history to date. There hadn't been rain or snow for a couple of months, and the open space lands became tinder, with 100-mph winds creating the perfect conditions for this kind of tragedy.

A MOST TREASURED POSSESSION

One afternoon in the Kapahi-based home where Grant and I had lived, I had gotten Grant settled on the toilet in the bathroom near the kitchen. A good friend had made a handicapped-accessible shower and toilet to accommodate Grant's wheelchair and both of us. Because homes aren't very large out there, it was a stone's throw from the kitchen and sink where I was washing our lunch dishes. I gave Grant his privacy; he was an earshot away in case he needed any help.

From out of nowhere, Grant said in the sweetest voice, "Honey, do you want my ponytail when I die?"

I nearly dropped the dish I was holding but collected myself and my thoughts in a quick moment and responded, "Yes, I would love to have your ponytail when you die."

It was the most unusual question. I had no idea what I was going to do with the ponytail. Once Grant retired, he had decided to grow his short, business-styled hair into longer locks reminiscent of his "vagabond hippie" days, as I liked to call them.

After Grant passed away, before they took his body, I put his ponytail into a braid, freshly washed from the night before. I cut it off and I still have it carefully placed in a plastic bag and in a special box for safekeeping. It is one of my most treasured possessions, a part of him that I'll have with me always. It represents his personal self-expression because he lost most of that during his illness. When he left corporate America, he decided he was never cutting his hair again. And then he got a tribal tattoo around his ankle with my name woven into it, a tribute to me. He got the tattoo on his right ankle, the same foot where his ALS weakness was first experienced.

After the Marshall Fire, when I had the chance to reflect upon what I would have been most impacted by—and missed, with our home and all of its contents—I immediately thought of Grant's braid. Not my passport, jewelry, or my lifetime collection of Christmas ornaments from around the world. And the special camphor wood art "urn," which I kept after scattering Grant's ashes in two different places of the world, that is still prominently placed on a shelf in my office, next to my dog Syd's ashes. I thought about this especially when people talked about what they worried about not having most. Why were people so concerned about not having the ashes of their loved ones? I think this is because there is something sacred about keeping your loved one's ashes in safe possession. As if you are protecting them or thinking that perhaps they are still attached to us in some way. But more likely, it's that we are still attached to them and what they represent, our loved one in human form. And people did not want to let go of that person they had loved once again.

INTO THE DEEP: THE HARMONIC EGG EXPERIENCE

I decided to use a unique relaxation experience while writing my book. It is called the Harmonic Egg® of Boulder County (harmonicegg.com). The owner of this particular egg, Mary Hastings, was in a networking group I joined during the 2020 pandemic. She gave me an experience for my birthday on June 4, 2021. I didn't realize how special this gift would be.

On my birthday, I typically reflect upon my life and how far I've come. This year was no different, at 53 years old and making the decision to finally take on writing this book. I had just received the "Solo Business of the Year" award from the Superior Chamber of Commerce and felt grateful and proud of my accomplishments in building my business over the past three years.

The Harmonic Egg is unlike anything I've experienced. You sit in an anti-gravity chair placed in the center of an egg-like therapeutic chamber. Colored light and music combinations have been created using the synchronized healing powers of sound and color. Intention plays an active role, interacting with the sound and color energetically and harmonically on a cellular level. There actually is a science behind the light and sound. Sound and light are considered ancient healing, older than our current medical model. The relaxation chamber appears to function in a realm where subatomic particles remain in contact with one another regardless of distance or time. I've referenced a book about it in my resources section below. The following is my first experience in the Harmonic Egg.

After a while spent meditating to the soulfully beautiful music of violins, I began to see a vision in my mind's eye. Grant came up to me dressed in his tux, looking as he did at our wedding, but completely unencumbered and walking without a cane. I sensed he didn't have ALS. As, in my mind's eye, I looked down at my hands in my lap, I saw that I was wearing my wedding dress. Grant gracefully took my hand and pulled me up to him in an embrace and began to slow dance with me to the beautiful song I was hearing, for what seemed to be the entire duration of that song. No words were exchanged between us, simply pure joy. When the song ended, my experience of being with Grant faded away and then another vision filled my mind's eye, including my grandma holding and rocking me as a baby.

As I exited the egg afterward, I asked Mary, "Has anyone ever told you they connected with someone from the other side while in here?" and she responded "No, no one has ever said anything about that." I decided to keep this dream-like experience with Grant and my grandma to myself because, well, I didn't realize I had that powerful of an imagination. I'd had the most incredible experience, and I thought, *Maybe I was dreaming while awake.*

I got in my car and drove through the parking lot with all of this fresh in my mind. As I did, I turned on the radio. I couldn't believe my ears. Our song, "In Your Eyes" by Peter Gabriel, came on! In that instant, I immediately knew it was Grant from the other side, somehow connecting with me in those special moments. Once again, however many years later, he had given me a birthday gift that was so hard to believe. I suddenly thought, *Why wouldn't he? Haven't I finally realized that time and again Grant's spiritual being is larger than this life?*

I kept this to myself for quite some time, as another cherished experience from the afterlife. Because Grant is larger than this life. And he always will be, just like we all will be someday. Although now Grant is my best friend on the other side, no longer my husband. I've been at peace with this for a very long time now and I think he is, too.

How lucky am I to have found a lasting love twice in my life? I don't take for granted that I have had, for more than 10 years now, an amazing and wonderful husband, Shawn. And how fortunate I am that Shawn has been able to hold this space with me, whether he has been completely conscious of this or not. It takes a special partner to be able to live with the memory of a deceased spouse. Not everyone does it well. But I've been fortunate. Shawn has respect for and knows Grant will always have a special place in my heart. Even though he may not know about all of these mystical experiences…at least not until he reads this book.

OVER THE RAINBOW

REFLECTION

Many times throughout Grant's illness I would pray to God, bargaining for Grant's health and the ability to start over again. I would tell God that He could take everything we had, leaving us nothing but the clothes on our backs to start over. And he could take those too, if he wanted them. As if bargaining and negotiating would give us Grant's health and our life back!

In light of the Marshall Fire, having seen people who have experienced leaving with only the clothes they wore and being completely humbled into a new beginning, I wondered, *Was this what I was ultimately bargaining for?* The bargaining that goes over and over in our minds when we lose what is most precious to us is hard to explain, yet very real when you think God may be listening and of course, He or She or They should have control over this situation if they are all-powerful, right?

I was angry at God for months and then for years. Couldn't They do something to help this situation? What I realized over time is that They did, and this is what I refer to as "rainbows." Those people, places, signs, and experiences that show up when you need them most. Like this young woman who walked into the Taro Fields clothing store one day. In our brief conversation, she was wiser than her years, telling me exactly what I needed to hear about having a better attitude that morning. It gave me the perspective I desperately needed to go home after work and not just make it through another day, but to actually make it a better one, filled with more love and harmony. I experienced profound gratitude for this angel encounter. I knew I wasn't alone.

I was able to witness and participate firsthand in supporting my community during the aftermath of the fires. There were so many needs, but our community pulled together to support and help each other—from the Soup Brigade bringing food to people, to food trucks, and businesses sponsoring Lasagna Night, to donation centers and colleagues of mine who bought a moving van, collecting clothing, furniture, and more for people who had

THE ERUPTING VOLCANO: UNBELIEVABLE LOSSES

nothing as they moved into vacant apartments and homes. It was awe-inspiring to see how our communities came together. We all need each other, and love helps to rebuild lives.

Have you ever noticed that sometimes it takes a while to see a rainbow form, to most fully recognize its vibrant range of colors? Sometimes there is a hint of a rainbow, hiding behind the clouds that maybe we don't see at all, unless we're wearing those polarized sunglasses. How can we see the colors and beauty through the intensity of our own loss and emotions? By having gratitude for what we do have and how we have been blessed in each moment.

Self-Reflection

Review and share your own collective community grief story in the *Over the Rainbow Companion Journal*.

How can you build a stronger community, connections, and supportive relationships? Think about an experience, idea, or time in your life when you and your community came together:

1. COVID-19 loss

2. Black Lives Matter: police brutality and shootings

3. Mass shootings: too many to name; violence in America

4. Natural disasters: fires, hurricanes, floods, earthquakes

5. Any other experience that has changed your life and the world we live in

THE ERUPTING VOLCANO: UNBELIEVABLE LOSSES

CHAPTER PLAYLIST/GUIDED MEDITATIONS

- "Everything I Wanted," Billie Eilish
- "Unstoppable," Sia
- "Titanium," David Guetta and Sia
- "Song for a Winter's Night," Sarah McLachlan (Gordon Lightfoot)
- For guided meditations, visit SheilaClemenson.com.

RESOURCES

- *Ambiguous Loss: Learning to Live with Unresolved Grief*, Pauline Boss
- *Burnout: The Secret to Unlocking the Stress Cycle*, Emily Nagoski, Ph.D., and Amelia Nagoski, DMA
- *How to Be an Antiracist*, Ibram X. Kendi
- *White Fragility: Why It's So Hard for White People to Talk About Racism*, Robin DiAngelo
- *You Are Your Best Thing: Vulnerability, Shame Resilience, and the Black Experience*, edited by Tarana Burke and Dr. Brené Brown
- *Unlocking The Ancient Secrets to Healing: Why Science is Looking to the Past for the Future of Medicine*, Gail Lynn

CHAPTER 10

Over the Rainbow: Gratitude, Resilience, and Joy

"Gratitude is a powerful catalyst for happiness. It's the spark that lights a fire of joy in your soul."

—*Amy Collette*

"Nourish what makes you feel confident, connected, contented. Opportunity will rise to meet you."

— *Oprah Winfrey*

"When the flower opens, the bees will come."

— *The poet Kabir*

LIVING IN ABUNDANCE

Living in spiritual abundance and gratitude has been a blessing in my life. By becoming more consciously aware of my actions, emotions, and impact on others, I've been able to stay in a more calm and peaceful inner space. I can access a higher vibration of positivity and love by being true to what really matters—the people I love. Standing in my integrity and walking my talk helps me build trust with others and is the foundation of everything I do.

By staying true to myself and others as a conduit for information, resources, understanding, love, and support, I show up as a coach, confidante, and a lightworker. While writing this book it has been important for me to keep my energy high by taking care of myself, being supported by others, holding true to my boundaries, and making time for my own creative process. I had to recognize my challenges of being distracted and not present with the people in my life, so that I can be more conscious to show up stronger in my higher spiritual self, closer to the version of who I want to be in this world. I'm always a work in progress.

ARCHANGELS, GUARDIAN ANGELS, AND SPIRIT GUIDES

Over the Rainbow: From the Depths of Grief to Hope is the grief book I wish I'd had after Grant died over 20 years ago. This book is a spiritual calling. I have felt strongly guided and supported by God/Goddess/Great Spirit, the Archangels, my guardian angels, spirit guides, deceased loved ones, and especially my deceased husband, Grant. I know I'm being supported as a lightworker on this journey. It might be hard for some to believe that Archangel Michael comes to me and makes his presence known with flashes of electric cobalt-blue light that suddenly catch my eye in a glimmer or play of light with mirrors or windows. Sometimes I sense that he is standing guard behind me, especially as I write at my computer. I trust that he has my back, especially when I'm feeling emotionally vulnerable while writing the most difficult parts of this book. I was thoughtful about including these metaphysical experiences that keep us connected with something bigger than us, including our loved ones on the other side. It might seem like a taboo subject, one to think about but not mention openly to others. Well, I guess I'm coming out of the "woo-woo" closet, because I'm inspired when I'm connected with these experiences that cannot be explained.

One day when I worked remotely, like most of us these days, and was taking a pee break (the humor is not lost on me that I was sitting on the toilet!), I noticed a slight glistening of light in front of me on our plain, light-gray wall. I looked up at the skylight to see what was making this illusion, perhaps snow or ice hitting the sunlight just right. But I didn't see any snow, ice, or condensation, which is important because I live in Colorado where we get plenty.

When I looked back at the wall, I noticed a faint cobalt blue around the edges of a shimmering light play. Suddenly, I could see a distinct outline of a pair of large resting wings, shimmering in a faint play of light. I was in awe! I looked more closely, noticing the patterns. I have a small parrot and I'm very familiar with the nature of wings. Yes, this is what it looked like! I rubbed my eyes, wondering if what I was seeing was in fact Archangel Michael. I do believe it was!

I believe that we're not alone and that we have the support of our guardian angels, spirit guides, and even the Archangels, if we ask for their presence, support, and guidance. Perhaps all we need to do is ask for what we need in support of the highest good of ourselves and others, listen, and then pay attention, feeling blessed and in awe when it shows up. I feel a soulful bond with my guardian angels, and I believe Grant in his spiritual essence is one of them. He supports and helps me from the other side.

Do we really think we need to do this life alone without help from the other side? This may be God/Goddess/The Universe/Great Spirit/Source Energy, or other angels and guides. Perhaps when we surrender to not needing to be the ones in control 24/7, this is when the real magic happens.

MESSAGES FROM SPIRIT GUIDES

I have had so many experiences while writing this book that they have become unquestioned and regular occurrences in my life. This can be good fun, like when I heard the song, "Oh, Oh Sheila" by Ready for the World while I was grocery shopping the other day. Or when the TV turned on by itself or the lights flickered to get my attention, as happened over the past two days. I'm near the end of my book and knew someone was trying to get my attention. I was lying in bed and obviously someone thought I needed to get to work!

SOUND & VIBRATION

My experiences in the Harmonic Egg were different every time I entered it. Before I got into the egg, I would set an intention to connect with my angels, spirit guides, and deceased loved ones. I felt at peace and in a deep state of relaxation while inside. On occasion, I would even notice no pain, especially if I had a slight headache before I got in. Sometimes nothing in particular would come to me, or I would fall asleep and trust that whatever messages I needed came to me in that session. I experienced pure relaxation as I imagined the Kalalau Valley, Ke'e Beach, Secret Beach, or the majestic Na Pali of Kauai. ("Heaven on Earth" is what I call Kauai.) Sometimes I would imagine myself flying above it all, as if I was a grand eagle feeling the lightness of the wind upon my wings taking higher flight.

At the end of one of my sessions, a Sarah McLachlan song came to mind. I started to hum it, but I couldn't remember the title, so I started to sing to myself. After my session, I needed to look it up; thank God for Google! It was "Song for a Winter's Night," the classic song by Gordon Lightfoot, sung by Sarah McLachlan. Was Grant sending me this song? He loved Gordon Lightfoot! As a sailor, he was intrigued by the wreck of the Edmund Fitzgerald, an American Great Lakes freighter that sank in Lake Superior during a storm on November 10, 1975. She is the largest ship to have sunk there.

When I visited Michigan in June of 2022, I enjoyed a beach walk with Grant's best friend Darv, Shawn, and Zoey, Shawn's and my dog. I walked further ahead, the wind blowing in my hair with my feet in the cold, fresh water of Lake Michigan. I asked Grant for any messages that I could give to Darv because I felt he needed to hear some encouragement from his dear friend. What I got instead was a song for me, "If You Could Read My Mind," another by Gordon Lightfoot. I thought that was hilarious, until I actually read the lyrics on my phone later.

Holy shit! What did the lyrics mean other than the obvious? The song is about loss, regret, loneliness, and grief. Gordon wrote it when he was getting divorced from his wife. Since I was writing my book at the time, the part about the paperback novel and the heartache of him being the hero, failing, and the heartache being too much to take, spoke so strongly to me. Wow, just wow! As much as I knew Grant was happy for me and the love I had found with Shawn in my life, he was also communicating that things didn't work out for us the way we had intended long ago.

Two days after this, on my birthday, 2022, Grant sent me a penny with the date 1992 (when we started dating). I found it in the center of the floor of Shawn's and my camper van. Then I saw a "Grantland" flag pass us from the corner of my eye as drove down a highway between Elk Rapids and Charlevoix, Michigan. Of course I did! Grant is always full of little surprises.

HO'OKIPA

On my most recent visit to Kauai in September 2022, I wanted to visit Ke'e Beach again, one of my favorite places on the island. While there, I felt called back to an ancient *heiau* (temple) located nearby, the one I was blessed to experience with A.K. on our Kauai adventure after Grant's death in 1999. I felt inspired to reconnect with the sacred land of my ancestors from what I believe is another life. Since my first visit to Kauai, I have believed that I've lived many lives there; I've experienced visions of this in past life regression.

As my friend Terri and I walked along the trail to Kalalau Valley, we found the *heiau*. I asked for permission to enter this sacred land and offer the gift of a song, "Beautiful Kauai." Terri and I decided to sit for quiet time to reflect and meditate, more fully connecting with the *mana* of this sacred place. In silence, I chose a larger lava rock to rest upon with a dramatic view of the ocean waves trundling upon the shore. Suddenly I heard a word spoken in my head, in a deep Hawaiian male voice chanting, "*Ho'okipa! Ho'okipa! Ho'okipa!*" I didn't know what the word meant at that time. It is a Hawaiian cultural tradition that you treat guests with honor, as they are a part of the *ohana*, and *ho'okipa* is a welcoming offering of hospitality. Although I didn't know this at the time, I did feel embraced and welcomed. I experienced the most comfortable sanctuary while resting and meditating. As I opened my eyes after absorbing the *mana* of the experience, I saw two orange butterflies in a dance with one another above my head, swirling around while rising together. This made me smile with complete joy. I was blessed and honored to be welcomed back to my Kauai home.

SPRING GARDENING

After more than 20 years since Grant died, it is no wonder I don't have an immediate recollection of certain memories. But I have been reminded of them during certain events, as I'll describe in this story and the next.

I was excited to plant flowers in the planters on my deck this spring. It was an unusually cold winter, even for Colorado. I don't have a green thumb; that is my husband, Shawn's, area entirely. However, I was ready to do this. After successfully planting my first bunch, I needed to move the compost bin, and instead of doing it in the correct way, I didn't put the top back on. As I moved it, the lid swung down, and I tripped on the lid, falling hard onto the brick landing. I sliced my finger on God knows what, bruised my ankle, and scraped my knee with what would be a good scab when it finally healed.

I was fortunate to have my personal EMT on hand. Shawn brought me upstairs to bandage me up and ensure I didn't get infected, by pouring and slathering solutions that stung nicely. As I waited for him to get supplies, I started laughing hysterically. Shawn asked, "Are you all right in there, or did you hit your head, too?"

When he came into the bathroom, I told him, "When Grant walked with his cane and someone looked at him a little longer or asked what was going on, he would say, 'Bizarre gardening accident.' And I just had one!" The humor wasn't lost on me that I remembered this, especially while writing this book and trying to describe Grant's sense of humor and how witty he was. Shawn was amused by the story, but not by my clumsy shenanigans. I wasn't allowed to plant anything else and needed to take a time out.

INTO THE DEEP: RISE UP

I will always remember what is most important in life, and yet with each passing day there are times I get caught up in the little things that don't really matter. How can I live from a more conscious place? Death is a profound teacher. Grief changes and transforms us, with experiences and memories that continue to show up often by surprise, another rogue wave.

In my final day of writing this last chapter, I asked everyone—God/Goddess/Great Spirit, the Archangels, my guardian angels, spirit guides, deceased loved ones—to come in for the highest good of all to help me finish what I had started more than a year and half earlier.

As I reviewed my chapters, I noticed the song "Rise Up" by Andra Day in the playlist of Chapter 3, about becoming a more conscious caregiver. I realized I hadn't seen the video, so I took a moment to look it up on my phone. I had no idea what to expect when I watched the official, "Inspiration Version," which I would highly recommend you do right now and then continue reading this.

To my surprise, it was like watching my life unfold exactly the way I had helped care for Grant. The way she helped him out of bed, the way she showered him. That he wanted to take her out on a date was priceless. I cried hard for the first time in a long time, thinking about the experience we lived every day for years. This is exactly how I felt! Andra was singing the words I lived.

I had pushed a deep, emotional experience so far down the rabbit hole of my mind that I didn't access it until I saw this video. While Grant was in the ICU two months before he died, there was a morning I had forgotten about. I was supposed to meet Grant in his ICU room each day, but I was running about 90 minutes late on this particular day because I needed to talk with his family about his health issues and what he was experiencing. It took so much longer than I had expected, and I didn't call Grant to let him know. We didn't have cell phones in 1999 like we do now, plus I figured he was relaxing and hopefully getting more sleep than he'd had in a while.

When I walked into his room, he was livid with me. Normally he was soft-spoken due to the difficulty of pushing the air from his diaphragm to communicate verbally. But this time, Grant yelled at me as loud as he could muster, "Get the fuck out of here and I don't want to see you!"

I had no idea what was going on, although I knew I was late and he was upset. I found out later that Grant had decided he was going to surprise me with a date.

He had arranged for food to be delivered and we were going to sit out on the terrace. The ICU nurses were helping him to make it happen. I'd had no idea he planned to do this. He continued to yell at me, "Get the fuck out of here!" Flustered, I left and drove to the west side of the island, to Waimea. I was an emotional train wreck, crying, devastated, and angry at myself. I had no idea if he would ever forgive me, or even still be alive from his breathing issues, when I returned to the hospital. I couldn't believe I had disappointed him so deeply. I hoped he could forgive me.

I decided to stop by his hospital room a couple of hours later. When I walked in, Grant was talking to one of the ICU RNs. She came out of the room when she saw me. Before I walked into the private suite, she said he was telling her stories about the day he married me and how beautiful I was. He was crying to her that he didn't want to die and lose me. When I came into his room, we both had tears in our eyes. I told him that I was so sorry, and I loved him so much and didn't mean to disappoint him.

This beautiful man who was trying with all his might to recover from aspiration pneumonia in the ICU had planned a date with me as a surprise. The "Rise Up" video took me back to that day. It doesn't matter how much time has passed. Our grief has layers, and the rogue waves can still surprise us, like they did for me, 24 years later. I believe I was supposed to share this story with you at this point in finishing the book. This is a beautiful way to show you how God/Goddess/the Great Spirit shows up in our lives. I don't think we are ever alone. I believe we are supported through life and our grief process in ways we don't yet realize, which bring us exactly what we need for our personal healing process and highest good.

REFLECTION

What is the stage of "acceptance" in grief? How do we come to terms with what our life is without our loved ones? I hope you see that moving forward is a process, and there is hard work involved in processing your emotions while holding on to your loved one's memory yet creating a new life for yourself. You will continue to have your own special relationship with them, if this is something you want. And if not, that is OK, too.

I hope by sharing the mystical experiences that have surprised me in the moment, giving me a sense of awe and wonder, you might have your own experiences to reflect upon. My hope is that you will be surprised in pleasant ways by these "rainbows" in your daily life. Because maybe your loved one is using a different language to communicate with you from the other side.

I ask my clients, "How do you want to spend your valuable time every day?" Because no matter how much time we have or how long we live, it's still short. So, we need to make it count. I have been given the greatest gift of seeing the big picture. What is really important in this life will be different for each person, based upon their values and what they treasure and hold most dear. The choices between career and professional goals, paying the bills, saving for the future, and living your meaningful purpose—everything we love and the things that get our attention in a day—are often a challenge. Somehow, we need to find balance to more fully live our best life. The difficulty is between being more in balance or out of balance; balance is not a destination, but a continuum and a daily journey. Trust in your ability to move forward one step at a time, living each day in gratitude. Gratitude builds resilience. Resilience brings joy, and this special blessing is right in front of you.

I value gratitude, love, kindness, relationships, humor, teamwork, connectedness, positivity, and empathy. By incorporating my values and strengths into my work and professional career, I know I will stay on the right path for me. I trust that where I need to be and who I need to support will come in. I trust that this book will reach whomever it needs to connect with, and my hope is they will read it when they need it most. I feel empowered as a messenger to share my experiences and insights, and to perhaps even open the minds of others to new perspectives, helping others see things in a different way. The humanness of life is heavy and limiting, but when we open ourselves up to the spiritual side of life, we nurture our souls in a higher vibration to fly with the angels, over the rainbow.

OVER THE RAINBOW: GRATITUDE, RESILIENCE, AND JOY

ALOHA

Aloha means hello and goodbye, I love you, and so much more. The *aloha* spirit is a Hawaiian way of living, the guiding power of love in one's heart that gives of itself. Living *aloha* is at the core of one's being: living into the values of honesty, truthfulness, patience, kindness, humility, and harmony. It is a sincere desire to share the beauty, serenity, and love that is Hawai'i. I hope you have felt this offering of *aloha* in my book. My wish is that you experience this magical place of being within yourself, if you haven't already. Perhaps someday you'll take your own adventure to the Hawaiian Islands and find your very own Secret Beach.

A HUI HOU

Until we meet again…you can always find me at SheilaClemenson.com.

Self-Reflection

Trust in your ability to move forward, living each day in gratitude, resilience, and joy.

- ❀ What "rainbows" do you experience in your daily life? Some of these experiences might be a favorite song or meaningful songs (pay special attention to the lyrics) that play anywhere at just the right time; familiar smells, like a favorite flower or someone's cologne; objects showing up in a place you wouldn't expect; meaningful animal totems, like butterflies, dragonflies, hawks, eagles, turtles; meaningful numbers appearing on clocks and license plates; words on license plates; and pennies/money, to name a few. You will know what is most special between you and your deceased loved one.

- ❀ How are you building your life without your loved one(s)?

- ❀ How do you hold on to their memory and continue to have your own special relationship with them?

- ❀ Explore how to look for mystical experiences, signs, and new ways of communicating with your loved ones. How do we bring more spiritual experiences into our life? By being open to new experiences; being in nature, meditation, and prayer; and anything you can do that increases your vibration. You can think positive thoughts and say affirmations to yourself. By believing in hope and love and being grateful for what you have. There are many ways—explore your world. Find a favorite place to meditate and connect with this beautiful planet, even if it's only in your mind's eye and imagination. See how real you can make this experience for yourself. Nurture your soul and your senses.

❀ Explore practicing living in gratitude and the way of living *Aloha*.

CHAPTER PLAYLIST/GUIDED MEDITATIONS

- ❀ "If You Could Read My Mind," Gordon Lightfoot
- ❀ "Rise Up," Andra Day, Official Music Video, Inspiration Version
- ❀ "Diamonds," Rihanna
- ❀ "Adventure of a Lifetime," Coldplay
- ❀ "Over the Rainbow," Judy Garland
- ❀ "It's a Wonderful World," Louis Armstrong
- ❀ "Somewhere Over the Rainbow/What a Wonderful World," (2007) Israel "Bruddah Iz" Kamakawiwo'ole
- ❀ For guided meditations, visit SheilaClemenson.com.

RESOURCES

- *The Art of Happiness: A Handbook for Living,* His Holiness The Dalai Lama and Howard C. Cutler, M.D.
- *The Gratitude Connection: Embrace the Positive Power of Thanks,* Amy Collette
- *Mana Cards: The Power of Hawaiian Wisdom,* Catherine Kalama Becker, Ph.D., and Doya Nardin

REFERENCES

CHAPTER 1

- *Atlas of the Heart*, Brené Brown, Ph.D., MSW
- *The Grief Recovery Handbook*, John W. James and Russell Friedman
- *On Grief and Grieving*, Elisabeth Kübler-Ross, M.D., and David Kessler
- *Visions, Trips, and Crowded Rooms*, David Kessler
- *Grief.com*—David Kessler

CHAPTER 2

- *365 Days of Understanding Your Grief: Daily Readings for Finding Hope and Healing Your Heart*, Alan D. Wolfelt, Ph.D.
- *Grief One Day at a Time: 365 Meditations to Help You Heal After Loss*, Alan D. Wolfelt, Ph.D.
- *Understanding Your Grief: Ten Essential Touchstones for Finding Hope and Healing in Your Heart*, Alan D. Wolfelt, Ph.D.
- *The Wilderness of Grief: Finding Your Way*, Alan D. Wolfelt, Ph.D.

CHAPTER 3

- ❀ *The Caregiver's Companion: Words to Comfort and Inspire*, Betty Clare Moffatt
- ❀ *Companioning the Bereaved: A Soulful Guide for Caregivers*, Alan D. Wolfelt, Ph.D.
- ❀ The Working Daughter, a Facebook Group
- ❀ *Tuesdays With Morrie: An Old Man, a Young Man and Life's Greatest Lesson*, Mitch Albom
- ❀ *Ask the Body and Treat the Priority*, Molly Jones, L.Ac.— Acupuncturist and Vibrational Medicine
- ❀ *A Touch of Hope: The Autobiography of a Laying-on-of-Hands Healer*, Dean and Rochelle Kraft

CHAPTER 4

- ❀ *A Return to Love*, Marianne Williamson
- ❀ "The Call to Courage" Dr. Brené Brown's TED Talk on vulnerability
- ❀ *Daring Greatly: How the Courage to Be Vulnerable Transforms the Way We Live, Love, Parent and Lead*, Brené Brown
- ❀ *You Are a Badass: How to Stop Doubting Your Greatness and Start Living an Awesome Life*, Jen Sincero

CHAPTER 5

- ❀ *Illuminata: A Return to Prayer*, Marianne Williamson
- ❀ *The Grief Recovery Handbook: The Action Program for Moving Beyond Death, Divorce and Other Losses, Including Health, Career and Faith*, John W. James and Russell Friedman, Founders of The Grief Recovery Institute. *griefrecoverymethod.com*

REFERENCES

- Information and guidance on the practice of *ho'oponopono*:
- self-i-dentity-through-hooponopono.com
- self-i-dentity-through-hooponopono.com morrnahs-questions-and-answers
- self-i-dentity-through-hooponopono.com/free-videos
- *The Book of Ho'oponopono: The Hawaiian Practice of Forgiveness and Healing*, Luc Bodin, M.D., Nathalie Bodin Lamboy, and Jean Graciet

CHAPTER 7

- *The Five Love Languages*, Gary Chapman
- *The Relationship Cure: 5-Step Guide to Strengthening Your Marriage, Family and Friendships*, John M. Gottman, Ph.D. and Joan DeClaire
- *The Seven Principles for Making Marriage Work,"* John M. Gottman, Ph.D., and Nan Silver
- *Ask and It Is Given: Learning to Manifest Your Desires*, Esther and Jerry Hicks (The Teachings of Abraham), abraham-hicks.com
- *Super Attractor: Methods for Manifesting a Life Beyond Your Wildest Dreams*, Gabrielle Bernstein

CHAPTER 8

- *Finding Your Own North Star: Claiming the Life You Were Meant to Live*, Martha Beck
- *Steering By Starlight: The Science and Magic of Finding Your Destiny*, Martha Beck
- *What Color is Your Parachute? A Practical Manual for Job-Hunters and Career-Changers*, Richard N. Bolles

- *Living on Purpose: Straight Answers to Life's Tough Questions*, Dan Millman
- *The Art of Work: A Proven Path to Discovering What You Were Meant to Do*, Jeff Goins

CHAPTER 9

- *Ambiguous Loss: Learning to Live with Unresolved Grief*, Pauline Boss
- *Burnout: The Secret to Unlocking the Stress Cycle*, Emily Nagoski, Ph.D., and Amelia Nagoski, DMA
- *How to Be an Antiracist*, Ibram X. Kendi
- *White Fragility: Why It's So Hard for White People to Talk About Racism*, Robin DiAngelo
- *You Are Your Best Thing: Vulnerability, Shame Resilience, and the Black Experience*, edited by Tarana Burke and Brené Brown
- *Unlocking The Ancient Secrets to Healing: Why Science is Looking to the Past for the Future of Medicine*, Gail Lynn

CHAPTER 10

- *The Art of Happiness: A Handbook for Living*, His Holiness The Dalai Lama and Howard C. Cutler, M.D.
- *The Gratitude Connection: Embrace the Positive Power of Thanks*, Amy Collette
- *Mana Cards: The Power of Hawaiian Wisdom*, Catherine Kalama Becker, Ph.D., and Doya Nardin

ACKNOWLEDGMENTS

WITH AN ABUNDANCE OF GRATITUDE for those of you who have touched my life and my book writing journey, whether you have been with me for a lifetime or a few moments or everything in between, you have supported and helped me to become the person I am today. I love my people and I wouldn't be here without you. I feel good about saying you know who you are in my life because I try my best to take the opportunity to share my appreciation for you for everything you have done to support me on my journey at different times in my life. If I measure my life by the relationships I have built over a lifetime, my heart is full, and I feel completely supported.

I want to thank my husband, Shawn, and my best friend on the other side, Grant, for being my life partners at different times on this journey. I wouldn't be the person I am today without both of you. My mom, brother, stepdaughters, extended family, and lifelong friends, including the "Biddies" (Lynae, Leslie and Karen), Dee, Anne-Kristine, Darv, Lori, Cindy, my Kauai Ohana, and chosen family of Michiganders, Coloradans, and Europeans for all you have brought to my life, I love you and you are my people. For all of my grief wellness and career coaching clients, you have supported my professional growth and development in ways you don't even know. Thank you for the insights you have given me in writing this book and the companion journal.

For my book journey, I would not have successfully completed this without you, my amazing book coaches, Amy Collette, Tisha Lin, and Vanessa Tavernetti. Amy, your ability to help me birth this book, in the way the stories needed to be told, is a testimony to the talents you bring as a professional with your business, Unleash Your Inner Author. Tisha, connecting with you at the beginning of my book journey was the wind that propelled me forward in confidence, feeling empowered to embark on this undertaking. Vanessa, bringing you in as my spiritual coach in support of connecting me with my intuition, and the soulful work we have done together, has given me the wings I needed to fly while grounding me at the same time. The three of you have been my book angels, and I'm so grateful to you.

For my cover and book design, I am blessed by the creativity and flexibility of my award-winning Book Designer, Victoria Wolf. You have captured the essence of grief and hope in my cover design and throughout my book by adding the special touches that take it to the next level.

I want to give special thanks to my following friends. Stephanie Miller, if it wasn't for your visioning presentation at our leads group, when you planted the seed for me to complete this book—the one thing on my bucket list that I would regret never doing—my gift to others would still be something I only hoped for someday. To my lifelong friend Deanne (Dee) McCarrison who came in at the last minute to save the day with the final review and proofreading, we will celebrate in a special way someday soon. my "sister" Lynae (Nae) Greely, as my reader in the early stages of the entire book, you gave me the confidence to move forward, more fully bringing the book to life and in more ways, as you know—you and John have gifted me in making this book a reality.

ACKNOWLEDGMENTS

Writing my book was a critical undertaking. However, launching it is the entire other half of the journey that most people don't tell you takes another army of angels with completely different skill sets. I have constantly said that I don't know what I don't know, and these people have helped me to fill in the gaps, offering their expertise in book launching, social media marketing and branding, public relations, podcast management, and the list goes on from here. Meredith and Nick at Marketing Maiden and Loveland Web Design, Michelle at Emagine Web Design, your gifts as marketing gurus, web designers, business owners, and content experts has been invaluable. I have loved being on this journey with you for many years. Heidi Howard, my friend, photographer, and branding expert with your unique talents to capture my essence through your camera lens and your coaching skills along the way. Erin Baer, book launch expert extraordinaire, you are "The Badass" and I'm so grateful for you, your expertise, and journey. Nathalie Baret, Publicist and PR Marketing Artist, you are the Real Deal, and you have found your calling as a gifted professional, making a difference with creative artists, musicians, and little ole me. Carrie Lubing, my podcast manager who has a special ability to highlight and pitch my unique qualities to find and connect with my audiences. Marla Press, my speaking coach, you've helped me to step into my authentic self while sharing my stories. Finally, to my Advance Readers, the feedback and experiences you have shared with me while reading my book have touched my heart and been priceless.

Fiona Wohlfarth and John Boggs, your support with social media and the audio book undertaking is a work in progress, and I'm grateful you have taken on the challenge. Our Superior Chamber Executive Director, Leslie Espinoza, and Event Manager, Renee Alaniz, your support in launching my book has been a gift, thank you! To have the full support of my community, including my Wednesday Leads Group, Women Rising, Trellis Colorado, Dress For Success Coaching Colleagues, and all of my professional networks, past and present supporting my success, you have my heartfelt gratitude.

OVER THE RAINBOW

To all of you—especially anyone I have been remiss in specifically mentioning your name—I hope you know who you are and the impact you have had on my life, my success is yours

www.ingramcontent.com/pod-product-compliance
Lightning Source LLC
Chambersburg PA
CBHW031319160426
43196CB00007B/578